FRANCE

Maxwell A. Smith, Guerry Professor of French, Emeritus
The University of Chattanooga
Former Visiting Professor in Modern Languages
The Florida State University

EDITOR

Fénelon

TWAS 542

François de Salignac de la Mothe-Fénelon
Archbishop of Cambrai

FÉNELON

By JAMES HERBERT DAVIS, JR.
University of Georgia

TWAYNE PUBLISHERS
A DIVISION OF G. K. HALL & CO., BOSTON

Published in 1979 by Twayne Publishers,
A Division of G. K. Hall & Co.
All Rights Reserved

Printed on permanent/durable acid-free paper and bound
in the United States of America

First Printing

Library of Congress Cataloging in Publication Data

Davis, James Herbert.
Fénelon.

(Twayne's world authors series ; TWAS 542 : France)
Bibliography: p. 177–81
Includes index.
1. Fénelon, François de Salignac de la Mothe-,
Abp., 1651-1715—Criticism and interpretation.
PQ1796.D3   848'.4'09   78-31470
ISBN 0-8057-6384-8

To Norma
who read it first

Contents

About the Author

James H. Davis, Jr. received his B.A., M.A., and Ph. D. degrees from the University of North Carolina at Chapel Hill. As a Fulbright scholar he also studied at the University of Paris in 1955–56. Since receiving his doctorate in 1963, he has taught at the University of Georgia where he presently holds the position of Associate Professor of French. Author of *Tragic Theory and the Eighteenth-Century French Critics* (1967), he has also contributed articles on French drama of the seventeenth and eighteenth centuries to scholarly journals.

Preface

It might appear at first glance that the life and works of Fénelon, well known to many readers as an essential part of that rich and varied tapestry we sometimes call the Age of Louis XIV, need scarcely be the subject of another volume. Although Fénelon no longer commands the attention of a large number of scholars and critics, his bibliography in quantity and quality is quite impressive. Despite this abundance of critical and biographical material, however, there have been to my knowledge only three books, intended for either the specialist or nonspecialist, written in English during the past forty years: J. Lewis May's *Fénelon* (1938), Katharine Day Little's *François de Fénelon* (1951), and Michael de la Bedoyere's *The Archbishop and the Lady* (1956). The first two works are marred to some extent by either a paucity of documentation, a tendency toward subjectivity, or a too rapid and superficial survey of some of Fénelon's major works. Bedoyere's volume, although quite readable, deals principally with the Quietist controversy. I feel therefore, that a study such as this—in which I have endeavored to depict Fénelon as neither saint nor heretic and in which I have allowed, as far as possible, his work to speak for itself—is in order. I do not expect the reader to love or even like the subject; I hope, nonetheless, that he will be able to gauge with some understanding the significance of Fénelon's contribution to Western literature and thought.

This study makes no claims to new discoveries or innovative approaches. I have drawn freely from the wisdom and scholarship of such specialists as Albert Cherel, Jules Lemaître, Ely Carcassonne, Jeanne-Lydie Goré, Louis Cognet, and Jean Orcibal, among others. In writing a book that might benefit the general reader, I have attempted to keep critical documentation and quotations within reasonable bounds. The numbers in parentheses refer to volume and page of the Paris edition of Fénelon's *Oeuvres complètes*, cited in the bibliography. The roman numerals used to identify the *Fables* and the *Dialogues des morts* in Chapter 3 correspond to those of this same edition. All translations, unless otherwise indicated, are my own.

The work of Fénelon is so extensive that it has been necessary to limit the scope of this volume to a study of those writings that best illustrate his achievement in the areas of pedagogy, theology, politics, and literature. Even so, I am quite aware that some readers may deplore my disregard of a favorite text or the omission of a certain topic. Perhaps it would have been desirable, for example, to include a chapter on the *Lettres spirituelles;* but it is my feeling that the basic message of that work is repeated to a large degree in the apologetic writings (which I discuss in Chapter 7), as well as in certain of the documents relative to Quietism. Also, because of limitations of space, I have written a somewhat abbreviated account of Fénelon's part in the Jansenist controversy. On the other hand, I have judged it fitting to begin with an introductory biographical chapter, which, along with the background material of Chapters 4 and 6, will provide the reader, I trust, with the information necessary for a better evaluation and appreciation of Fénelon.

JAMES H. DAVIS, JR.

University of Georgia

Chronology

1651   August 6: Birth in Périgord, near Sarlat, of François de Salignac de la Mothe-Fénelon, the second child of Pons de Salignac and his second wife, Louise de la Cropte de Saint-Abre. September: Louis XIV attains his majority.

1663–   Studies at the Université de Cahors.
1665[?]

1666[?]   Goes to Paris where he is enrolled in the Collège du Plessis.

1672–   Enters the Séminaire de Saint-Sulpice.
or
1673[?]

1674   Fénelon is ordained.
or
1675[?]

1675–   Fulfills duties in his parish of Saint-Sulpice.
1678

1677   Named doctor in theology by the Université de Cahors.

1678   Appointed Superior of the Congrégation des Nouvelles Catholiques, an institution founded for the instruction of Protestant women converted to Catholicism. He will hold this position until 1689.

1681   Fénelon is given, through his uncle, the Bishop of Sarlat, the benefice of Carenac.

1682   August 6: Birth of Louis XIV's grandson, the Duc de Bourgogne.

1683   Death of the Marquis Antoine de Fénelon (uncle).

1685–   October: Revocation of the Edict of Nantes. December:
1686   Fénelon chosen to head a mission for the conversion of Protestants in the provinces of Aunis and Saintonge. He remains there until July, 1686.

1687   March: Publication of the *Traité de l'éducation des filles*. May: Resumes his missionary work which he continues until July.

1688   October: Meets Madame Guyon for the first time. The *Traité du ministère des pasteurs* is published.

1689   August: Appointed preceptor to the Duc de Bourgogne.

1690–   Composition of the *Fables* and the *Dialogues des morts*.
1693[?]

1693   March: Elected to the Académie Française.

1694   July: The Issy Conferences begin. Fénelon composes the
         Lettre à Louis XIV[?]. *Le Gnostique de Saint Clément
         d'Alexandrie*[?].

1695   March: Fénelon signs the Issy articles. July: Consecrated
         by Bossuet as Archbishop of Cambrai. December: Madame
         Guyon is imprisoned at Vincennes.

1696   March: Composes the *Explication des Articles d'Issy*.

1697   January 25: Publication of the *Explication des Maximes des
         saints sur la vie intérieure*. March: Bossuet's *Instruction sur
         les états d'oraison* appears. April: Fénelon submits the
         Maximes for papal approval. August: Exiled to Cambrai.
         September 15: Fénelon's *Instruction pastorale sur le pur
         amour*.

1698   June: Publication of Bossuet's *Relation sur le quiétisme*.
         August: Fénelon's *Réponse à la Relation sur le quiétisme*.

1699   January: Deprived of his title and pension as preceptor.
         March 12: Papal condemnation (the brief *Cum Alias*) of the
         Maximes des Saints. April: Publication of *Télémaque*. Dis-
         grace of Fénelon. June: Four *Dialogues des Morts* (XXI,
         XXXVII, LXI, LXXIV) are published.

1700   November: Death of Carlos II of Spain.

1701–   War of Spanish Succession.
1713

1701   First of the *Mémoires concernant la Guerre de la Succession
         d'Espagne*.

1702   April and September: Fénelon has two interviews with the
         Duc de Bourgogne.

1704   Death of Bossuet. Fénelon begins his campaign against the
         Jansenists.

1707   *Discours pour le sacre de l'Electeur de Cologne*.

1708   Lille captured by the Allies. *Lettres sur l'autorité de l'Eglise*
         [?].

1709   The French defeated at Malplaquet.

1711   April: Death of the Dauphin. November: Fénelon and the
         Duc de Chevreuse compose the document that will be
         known as the *Tables de Chaulnes*.

1712   February 18: Death of the Duc de Bourgogne. Publication of Part I of the *Traité de l'existence et des attributs de Dieu.* (Part II will be published for the first time in 1718.)

1713   *Lettres sur divers sujets de métaphysique et de religion* (First printed edition, 1718). Beginning of correspondence with Houdar de La Motte, which will continue until December, 1714.

1714   Composes the *Lettre à l'Académie* (published, 1716). *Instruction pastorale en forme de dialogues sur le système de Jansenius.* August: Death of the Duc de Beauvillier.

1715   January 7: Fénelon dies at Cambrai.

CHAPTER 1

Life and Times

I Ancestry and Early Years

FRANÇOIS de Salignac de la Mothe-Fénelon was born on August 6, 1651, in the southwestern province of Périgord in his family's chateau which is located six miles from the town of Sarlat. His father, Pons de Salignac, whose first wife died in 1646, had married Louise de la Cropte de Saint-Abre in 1647; Fénelon was the second child of this union. Although poor, the Salignacs were aristocrats who traced their lineage as far back as the tenth century. In his middle years, Fénelon was to remind his brother that their family had counted among its members provincial governors, kings' chamberlains, a knight of the Order of the Holy Spirit, ambassadors, and high-ranking military officers.[1] In point of fact, his great-great-uncle, Bertrand, had served as ambassador to the court of Elizabeth I; and a maternal uncle, the Marquis de Saint-Abre, killed at Sintzheim in 1674, had held the rank of lieutenant-general. Numerous relatives had also been Bishops of Sarlat, including Fénelon's uncle, François de Salignac, appointed to that post in 1659. A latter-day descendant, Bertrand de Fénelon, was a friend of Marcel Proust and more than likely served as the model for that writer's character Saint-Loup-en-Bray in *A La Recherche du temps perdu.*

Very little is known of Fénelon's childhood and early education. His principal biographers have assumed that, being a frail child, he was tutored at home from eight until twelve years of age. The name of his preceptor, a certain Meneschié, has survived, and takes the credit for Fénelon's formative training in classical languages. In 1663 François was sent to study with the Jesuits at the Université de Cahors. Again, there is a lack of detail with regard to these early years, but it is believed that he studied humanities and philosophy, a program of study which was in no way different from the curriculum of his fellow classmates.

Fénelon's father died the year that he began his matriculation at the University of Cahors. In the absence of paternal influence and guidance, the young man's uncle, Antoine, Marquis de Fénelon, began to exert considerable bearing on his future education and career. The Marquis, an erstwhile soldier-swashbuckler-duellist turned devout member of a Catholic reform group we know well today as the Compagnie du Saint-Sacrement, had for years considered Paris his permanent residence; and to that city in 1666 he brought Fénelon to enroll in the Collège du Plessis. Concentrating on theology and philosophy, he entered a period of deep religious formation, influenced no doubt by Charles Gobinet, the principal of the school who discouraged the pursuit of pleasure and stressed the knowledge of self and of God. By the time Fénelon completed his two years at du Plessis, he was living "a life of pure spirituality."[2]

The Marquis de Fénelon continued to encourage his nephew in the ways of piety and devotion. No longer was there any question of the young man's future vocation, and it was decided that he should receive his training for the priesthood at Saint-Sulpice, a seminary which had been founded in 1641 by Antoine's intimate friend Jean-Jacques Olier. Fénelon began his studies there either in 1672 or 1673 under the direction of M. Tronson, the superior. During the time when the battle between Jansenists and Jesuits was raging, particularly during the 1650s, Saint-Sulpice was and remained a haven for quiet, pious men dedicated to the reaffirmation of the priestly calling. Theological polemics and philosophical debate were not their concerns; they were uncomplicated men devoted to spiritual perfection and humble virtue. The teaching and guidance of Tronson were to leave a lasting impression on Fénelon. Years later when he was far removed from court and city, he stated in a letter[3] to Pope Clement XI: "I congratulate myself on having had M. Tronson for my instructor in the Word of Life and having been formed under his personal care for the ecclesiastical state. Never was any man superior to him in love of discipline, in skill, prudence, piety, and insight into character" (7, 612–13).

II   The Priest and Missionary

The exact date of Fénelon's ordination is unknown, but tradition has it that it was either 1674 or 1675. According to Cardinal de Bausset's *Histoire de Fénelon*, he spent the next three years serving as priest in the parish of Saint-Sulpice, entrusted with the task of expounding the Scriptures on Sundays and holy days (10, 9). It is probable that he also performed the rather humble duties of teaching catechisms, hearing confessions, and ministering to the sick and the poor.

Fénelon, now in his mid-twenties, may have harbored other ambitions. Biographers and critics have referred time and again to one particular letter, usually dated October 9, 1675 ("All of Greece is opened before me. The Sultan retreats in terror. The Peloponnese draws the breath of liberty. The Church of Corinth blooms again. There the voice of the Apostle will be heard once more . . ."), in order to substantiate Fénelon's youthful zeal for evangelical work in the Levant. More than likely, this letter was written some ten or eleven years later.[4] At any rate, Fénelon's dream of missionary service in an exotic setting, where pagan and Christian worlds fused, was never to be realized. It was probably just as well; his frail health, as has been suggested, could not have met the demands of rigorous foreign service.[5]

Fénelon's years of parochial service did not, however, go unnoticed. His talent and his zeal had been observed by François de Harlay, the Archbishop of Paris; and in 1678, at the age of 27, he was named by that churchman to the position of Superior of the Congrégation des Nouvelles Catholiques (10, 10–11). It would also be just to assume that the influence of Fénelon's uncle may well have played a large part in the Archbishop's choice for the new appointment.

Les Nouvelles Catholiques was an institution that had been founded in 1634 by the Compagnie de la Propagation de la Foi for the instruction and rehabilitation of Protestant women recently converted to Catholicism. One of Fénelon's most severe critics, Onésime Douen,[6] has characterized the institution as a sort of horrible detention home where cruelties abounded and intolerance reigned. The home was but one manifestation of the government's program for Catholic unification and Protestant repression which had been intensified in 1669 by the passage of counter-edicts and prohibitions. Despite the eighteenth-century view of Fénelon as an enlightened spirit, it must be remembered that he was, like Louis XIV and most of the Catholic majority, sternly convinced that Huguenots were heretics; as such, he was strongly desirous of their conversion. At any rate, it is now known that Fénelon's duties at Les Nouvelles Catholiques were less administrative and more advisory.[7]

It is most difficult to picture him as any one other than a persuasive, spiritual mentor, well suited for teaching and guidance and little disposed to the idea of forced conversions and the horrors of conventual punishment. Fénelon's humane character was to be borne out by his attitudes and policies with regard to the second phase of his work with Protestant missions.

In October of 1685, the Edict of Nantes, Henry IV's great reform measure which assured Huguenots, among other things, freedom of worship, was revoked. It was the signal for another concentrated drive to make all loyal Frenchmen Catholic and to erase forever the taint of Calvinism. In December following the revocation Fénelon was chosen to head a mission designed to bring about the conversion of Protestants in the region around La Rochelle and Rochefort, that is, in the provinces of Aunis and Saintonge. This southwestern area of France had been for many years a Huguenot stronghold.

It was a difficult assignment. The stubborn and recalcitrant populace had in many instances been menacingly goaded to the point of conversion through the work of the dragoons, royal troops dispatched to second the efforts of the missionaries. Fénelon was opposed to such methods; fake conversions he could regard only with scorn. He deplored, moreover, the work of certain Jesuits, who, as he described to the Duchesse de Beauvillier, "speak of this world only in terms of fines and prison and of the other world only in terms of the devil and hell."[8] Fénelon preferred firm, but more gentle methods. Capable instruction by sympathetic priests and the distribution of New Testaments, as well as annotated translations of the Mass, were in part his answers to the problem.[9] After less than three months (in March, 1686), he confided to Bossuet: "Our converts are getting on a bit better, but the progress is slow. It is no small thing to change the feelings of an entire people."[10]

Fénelon's first mission ended in July, 1686, and in May of the following year he returned for further work. By the end of June, 1687, approximately a month before he concluded his assignment, he wrote to Seignelay, Louis XIV's minister: "I foresee that our work which begins to promise to bear great fruit will yield very little, unless it is maintained after us by workers stationed here for several years."[11] Fénelon was now prepared to leave this field to others; the experience for him "seems to have been largely disillusion, though it was no doubt a profound lesson in human nature not to be lost in the future."[12] In August, 1687, Fénelon returned to Paris to resume his work at Les Nouvelles Catholiques.

When Fénelon left Saint-Sulpice to take up his work at Les Nouvelles Catholiques, he had gone to live with his uncle Antoine in the Abbey of Saint-Germain-des-Près. Here in the entourage of his benefactor he met for the first time Bossuet, Bishop of Meaux. By 1683, the year in which Antoine died, it is assumed that Fénelon had been, for several years at least, a member of the Bishop's study group, an intimate circle of friends who gathered frequently at Germigny, Bossuet's country home. This decade of the 1680s was a period rich in associations and influences: under Bossuet's patronage Fénelon was to meet, among others, the Abbé Fleury, La Bruyère, Galland, Mabillon, and Pellisson. His early works, not only the *Réfutation du système du Père Malebranche (Refutation of the System of Father Malebranche)* but also the *Dialogues sur l'éloquence (Dialogues on Eloquence)*, the *Traité du ministère des pasteurs (Treatise on the Ministry of Pastors)*, and the *Traité de l'éducation des filles (Treatise on the Education of Girls)*, reflect the interchange of ideas of this coterie of new friends. Also during this era, probably around 1685, Fénelon wrote what some modern scholars consider to be the second part of his *Traité de l'existence de Dieu*, a work he would complete later at Cambrai.[13]

At approximately the same time as Fénelon was introduced to Bossuet he was, again thanks to his uncle, presented to the Duc de Beauvillier and the Duc de Chevreuse, his brother-in-law. These noblemen, both of whom had married daughters of Louis XIV's finance minister Jean-Baptiste Colbert, received Fénelon into their devout and serious-minded group which also included Madame de Maintenon (who became Louis XIV's morganatic wife in 1684) and the Duchesse de Mortemart, another of Colbert's daughters. It was for the Duchesse de Beauvillier that Fénelon composed his *Traité de l'éducation des filles*.

III *The Preceptorship*

On August 6, 1689, Louis XIV's grandson, the Duc de Bourgogne, celebrated his seventh birthday. As was customary for a royal child, he was to be separated at that time from his governess and placed under the supervision of a *gouverneur* who would be entrusted with the responsibility for his education and general welfare.

It was assumed that this official would be a courtier of distinction; there was little surprise, therefore, when the Duc de Beauvillier, already First Gentleman of the Chamber and special advisor to the King, was named to that post on August 16. Almost immediately he announced Fénelon as his choice for preceptor to the young prince.

Fénelon's elevation to this prestigious, coveted position was obviously a reflection of Beauvillier's friendship as well as an expression of esteem for the priest's pedagogical credentials as evidenced by the *Traité de l'éducation des filles*. Madame de Maintenon's very special regard for Fénelon seems also to have played a large part in the decision, for she is credited with securing the favorable endorsement of the king, otherwise not too well disposed toward the priest. Late that August Fénelon resigned his post at Les Nouvelles Catholiques and assumed his new duties amidst general approbation, bringing to the work at hand his reputation for patience, conscientiousness, eloquence, and charm. He chose as his assistants, those who would be directly concerned with the actual instruction, two of his closest associates, the Abbé Fleury who was named subpreceptor, and the Abbé Langeron who was to serve as reader.

Although Fénelon possessed great personal qualifications, he was faced, nonetheless, with an awesome task. It was more than apparent that the young Louis might one day rule France. Since the education of his father, the Dauphin, which had been directed by none other than Bossuet, was judged a dismal failure, there was all the more reason for Fénelon to summon forth the full measure of his intellectual and moral resources. From the beginning Fénelon realized that boredom, constraint, and cruelty could play no part in the educational process. Most of all, the lessons of the Duke, to the mind of the new preceptor, were to fit the needs of kingship; pedantry was to be banished from the classroom, and in its stead an intimate, pleasurable, and paternal atmosphere was to reign.

We have no formal record of Fénelon's academic program for the Duc de Bourgogne (and for his brothers, the Duc d'Anjou and the Duc de Berry, who came under the supervision of the preceptor in 1690 and 1691 respectively); but the *Mémoire* (c. 1696), drawn up by the Marquis de Louville, as well as two letters from Fénelon to Fleury (1695, 1696) provide us with a more than general notion of the curriculum in question (7, 517–24). The two major subjects studied were Latin, to be mastered and improved mainly through the preparation of *thèmes* (translations from French to Latin) and *versions* (translations from Latin to French); and history, to be studied from both secular and ecclesiastical standpoints. The natural sciences, physics, and modern foreign languages, strange though it may seem, were singularly neglected. Instruction in mathematics was in particular frowned upon, as it was feared that Louis "might easily have specialized in this" (7, 522).

To relieve the tedium of the day-to-day classroom regime and to complement the prescribed reading materials, Fénelon began to write for his young charge original compositions that would convey to him, in a pleasing and attractive manner, basic lessons in conduct and morality. His first effort along these lines was a series of prose apologues and tales, the *Fables*, designed to appeal to an eight-to-ten-year-old pupil. Next came the *Dialogues des morts (Dialogues of the Dead)*, Fénelon's transformation of the Lucianesque form into didactic conversations which exhibit a medley of history, mythology, and politics deemed suitable for a student ten years of age or older. He also offered to his student his version of *The Odyssey*, translating Books V through X (a précis was provided for the rest), and furnished him Latin translations of selected *Fables* by La Fontaine from Books I through VIII. Finally, probably sometime between the end of 1694 and 1696, Fénelon composed for the guidance and edification of young Louis the *Télémaque*, which remains one of the best known of his works.

IV *The Disciple of "Pure Love"*

By the time Fénelon began the composition of *Télémaque*, he was no longer just a talented, ambitious priest who, in the words of the well-known seventeenth-century memorialist Saint-Simon "had for a long time knocked at all the doors without having them opened."[14] As teacher, pulpit orator, and spiritual director, Fénelon's reputation had grown to the point that there appeared to be no doubt concerning his future success. In March, 1693, he was elected to the French Academy, and at Christmastime, 1694, Louis XIV gave him the important benefice of the Abbey of Saint-Valéry-sur-Somme with an income of fourteen thousand *livres*. These honors were followed by an even greater one: on February 4, 1695, Fénelon was named Archbishop of Cambrai.

There seems to be no real reason for suspecting the king of ulterior motives or of devious maneuverings in his decision to send Fénelon to Cambrai. After all, Louis had not seen the priest's acer-

bic, condemnatory *Lettre à Louis XIV* (did he ever, for that matter?); nor had he read *Télémaque*, which was not printed until 1699.
He was, in fact, quite generous in stipulating that Fénelon was to
retain the preceptorship, spending three months at court and the
remainder of the year in his new diocese. Madame de Maintenon,
on the other hand, was apparently the one most pleased to see
Fénelon depart. It was she who heard the distant rumblings of
scandal, who sniffed the acrid brewings of dissent among members
of the devout party. In order to keep the king ignorant of what was
really going on, it was better, she felt, that the new archbishop take
his leave without further ado.

To explain the motivations of Madame de Maintenon and to ex-
pose the events that would ultimately bring about a sudden reversal
of Fénelon's fortunes, it is necessary to retrace our steps. We must
return to the autumn of 1688, when, for the first time, at the home
of the Duchesse de Béthune-Charost Fénelon met Madame Guyon.
He had heard but knew little of this strange, devout widow, a new
disciple and advocate of a doctrine referred to as Quietism. It was a
religion of mysticism, of "pure love" as it would be called, that
stressed the abandonment of the self to God through passive contemplation and the cultivation of inner spiritual resources. For the
conservative wing of the church it was an alarming heresy, since it
obviously tended toward a neglect of ritual and a rejection of works.
In Spain the priest Miguel de Molinos (1640–1697) had been arrested in 1685 and subsequently condemned by the Inquisition in
1687 for his particular brand of Quietist views. Madame Guyon
herself, at the instigation of the Archbishop of Paris, François de
Harlay, had been confined to the Visitation Convent in the Rue
Saint-Antoine for eight months prior to that first meeting with
Fénelon. It is thanks to the intervention of Madame de Maintenon,
receptive to the petition of the amiable and devout Madame de
Miramion, who was much taken with the pious Madame Guyon,
that the latter was finally released.

Fénelon, on the other hand, was to all appearances little enchanted by this woman whose vagaries and misadventures before
she reached Paris and whose association with the controversial
Father La Combe smacked of scandal and moral turpitude. He was,
in fact, full of reserve. Madame Guyon sensed, however, that there
was "a total rapport" between two souls.[15] Soon he consented to
read her works, including the controversial *Moyen court et très*

facile de faire oraison (*Short and Easy Method of Prayer*, 1685), and
to correspond with her. Assuming at first that his role would be
primarily that of *directeur de conscience*, Fénelon gradually became
entranced with Madame Guyon's notion of the contemplative,
interior life. By Good Friday of 1689, he would write to her: "I think
of you very often, and I find myself more and more joined to you in a
general union of pure faith."[16] The two continued their correspondence until the end of 1689; meanwhile, they arranged secret
meetings and exchanged poems and songs, all of which would cause
even Fénelon's staunchest admirers to admit that there was something about this affair that was indeed silly and puerile. As one of
Fénelon's biographers has observed, there seemed to be "a secret
part of his nature which welcomed the simplicity, the relaxation, the
childlikeness involved in Madame Guyon's teaching."[17]

V   *Quietism on Trial*

Madame de Maintenon in her own way was also beguiled by
Madame Guyon and her new spirituality. She invited her to Saint-
Cyr, the school she had founded in 1686 for the daughters of im-
poverished nobles, for a series of devotional conferences. There
Madame Guyon was welcomed in particular by her cousin, Madame
de la Maisonfort, one of the Dames of that institution. Fénelon
would have preferred that "pure love" remain a doctrine accessible
only to an élite; it was his contention that this religion without tears
was not meant for just anyone. The opposite occurred, however,
and as the *Mémoires* of Madame du Pérou reveal, "Practically the
whole house became Quietist without knowing it. The talk was only
of pure love, *abandon*, holy indifference, and simplicity. Even
among the lay sisters and servants, it was always a question of pure
love. And some, instead of doing their work, spent their time reading Madame Guyon's books.[18]

It did not take Madame de Maintenon long to become worried
about Madame Guyon's disruptive influence at Saint-Cyr. What she
feared most was that news of the new spirituality and its foothold in
her revered institution would leak to the public, and that the taint of
scandal would be upon them. For a while, during 1691 and 1692,
she discreetly advised Madame de la Maisonfort to deemphasize the
Guyonian principles. Her advice, however, fell upon deaf ears. The
tension at Saint-Cyr continued to mount until finally, in desperation, Madame de Maintenon turned for aid to Godet Des Marais,

Bishop of Chartres and ecclesiastical superior of Saint-Cyr. The churchman began his investigations (probably in the autumn of 1692) with the result that Madame Guyon, in May of 1693, was asked to end her visits to the school.

Apprised of the situation, the Quietist forces quickly rallied. Madame Guyon now realized that an outsider, a disinterested party, should read her works and judge their orthodoxy. Probably because of the influence of Fénelon and the intervention of the Duc de Chevreuse, the choice of such a person fell upon Bossuet, who accepted the responsibility. He met with Madame Guyon in August of 1693 and again in Janauary of the following year. Meanwhile he agreed to read Madame Guyon's writings, a task that he laboriously completed sometime near the end of the winter of 1694. In her meetings with Bossuet, Madame Guyon seemed, outwardly at least, submissive enough. She was most certainly keeping her own counsel, despite the fact that she now feared that the Archbishop of Paris might be thinking of incarcerating her again. On the advice of Fénelon, she wrote to Madame de Maintenon in June, 1694, to request a hearing on the subject of both her doctrine and her morals. Madame Guyon's petition was granted, and thus began those meetings that were to be known as the Issy Conferences.

Bossuet, Noailles (at this time Bishop of Châlons), and Fénelon's revered mentor from Saint-Sulpice, the Abbé Tronson, were appointed as a panel of commissioners to conduct the investigation which began that July. It was decided that the deliberations would concentrate not on Madame Guyon's morals or lack thereof but on the question of orthodox mysticism. In other words, true Quietism was to be separated from the false and the heretical. Although Fénelon at the outset was not officially a judge, he contributed to the proceedings by furnishing certain documentation and annotated texts relative to the literature of mysticism. By February, 1695, shortly after his nomination for the archbishopric, Fénelon had come to play a more active role.

Bossuet had by the first of March drafted a report on the conferences in the form of thirty articles or statements. Fénelon found that number XXVII (denying that there is a necessary link between the gift of prophecy and a certain state of prayer) was inexact. Other articles, number IX and number XXIX, for example, he felt needed qualification.[19] Bossuet complied with his suggestions and for purposes of clarification and elucidation added four new ones. Fénelon was appeased and joined the other three in signing the report on March 10, 1675.

The Issy Articles amounted to little more than a compromise. While they reiterated the main obligations of the Christian, expressing thereby a kind of catechism, they remained imprecise concerning such burning questions as passive prayer or extraordinary states of prayer.[20] In essence, both Fénelon and Bossuet had achieved a victory of sorts: the former had succeeded in saving Quietism from outright condemnation; the latter had been able to show that Madame Guyon's doctrine tended—and dangerously so—to transcend certain basic truths.

VI *Controversy and Disgrace*

To all indications the Quietist Affair was settled. Madame de Maintenon, most certainly, could breathe more easily now, given the fact that Madame Guyon was tucked away in a convent at Meaux, and Fénelon was on his way to Cambrai to begin his new duties. For Bossuet, however, there were certain loose ends to be tied together. He had every intention of writing his own commentary on the Issy Articles, which was to take the form of a spiritual treatise. Fénelon, as late as December, 1695, believed that Bossuet still wanted him to collaborate on the project, since all along that had been the latter's implication. Two months later Fénelon learned that the work was to be, among other things, an impassioned attack on Madame Guyon, who by this time had been placed in the prison at Vincennes, and the errors of Quietism. Rather hastily then the archbishop began to prepare his own version of a commentary, calling it the *Explication des Articles d'Issy (Explanation of the Issy Articles)*. He must have felt that now he, and not his Quietist friend, would soon be forced to play the role of defendant.

When the manuscript of Bossuet's *Instruction sur les états d'oraison (Instruction on the States of Prayer)* reached Fénelon in July of 1696, he noticed, as soon as he opened its pages, that there were marginal citations from Madame Guyon's *Moyen court*. His reaction is expressed in a letter to the Duc de Chevreuse (July 24, 1696): "I am persuaded that he [Bossuet] is attacking at least indirectly in his work that little book. That is what makes it impossible for me to approve it [Bossuet's work]; and since I do not wish to read and then refuse to approve it, I am resolved to read none of it and to return it as soon as possible."[21] At that point he decided that he should write a work of his own, one that would more than sufficiently clarify his doctrinal position. He therefore began to compose the book that was to be his undoing, the *Explication des maximes des saints sur la vie intérieure (Explanation of the Maxims of the Saints on the Interior Life)*.

Fénelon's intention in writing the *Maximes* was not to defend Madame Guyon, but rather to formulate an apology for "pure love." Even before the Issy Conferences had begun, he felt that mysticism, even for those trained in theology, was a misunderstood, obscure doctrine. Many inexactitudes and misconceptions needed to be corrected; and to do so, Fénelon presented forty-five articles or points, each of which was divided and discussed under headings of "true" and "false." For his documentation and sources he used, as he had done in the midst of the meetings at Issy, the writings of Saint Teresa, Saint John of the Cross, Saint Catherine of Genoa, and Saint François de Sales, among others.

Before publishing the *Maximes*, Fénelon wanted to have the work read and approved by Noailles (who was now Archbishop of Paris). In mid-October, 1696, therefore, he sent him a copy. Noailles kept the text for about a month; and although he confided to the Duc de Chevreuse that the book was "too docile," he judged it "correct and useful."[22] He did suggest, however, that Fénelon make certain changes, and that he then submit the *Maximes* to M. Pirot, a doctor of the Sorbonne, for his scrutiny. Again a favorable reply was returned; Pirot did not hesitate to state that the book was "golden from start to finish."[23] Tronson later joined the others in voicing his approval of the *Maximes*.

It was Fénelon's agreement with Noailles that he would not allow his commentary to be printed until Bossuet's *Instruction* had appeared. The Duc de Chevreuse, who had assumed the responsibility for publishing Fénelon's work, convinced Noailles that if they delayed, Bossuet might find means of suppressing it. Thus the publication date was advanced, and the *Maximes* was ready for sale before February 1, 1697, a full month in advance of Bossuet's *Instruction*. It was the signal for the beginning of the last act of a drama that had begun almost a decade before.

Bossuet at this point wasted little time in denouncing the *Maximes* and declaring Fénelon's doctrine heretical. Louis XIV, finally brought up to date on what had transpired, was indignant and outraged when he learned of Fénelon's past association with

Madame Guyon and her strange sect. Noailles and Des Marais attempted to play the role of mediators, hoping that they could avert further trouble and prevent full-scale scandal. Des Marais even suggested the preparation of a new emended edition of the *Maximes*, but Fénelon no longer felt a compromise was possible. In his opinion he had but one recourse left. On April 27, 1697, Fénelon drafted a letter to Pope Innocent XII, in which he first explained why he had written the *Maximes* and then asked not to be condemned until his work was judged. The king reluctantly granted him permission to relay the document to the Papal Nuncio in Paris. That summer, before the end of July, Louis XIV decided to send his own message, dictated by Bossuet, to Rome. What he said in essence was that the *Maximes* had been judged by a large number of French prelates and theologians and found dangerous to the faith. On August 1, by royal decree, Fénelon was ordered to retire to his diocese at Cambrai and to remain there without returning to either Paris or the Court. Thus began an exile that was to last until his death in 1715.

Fénelon's banishment thus ensured Bossuet victory in the first phase of a battle that was now to shift its center of action from Versailles to Rome. The final triumph for the Bishop of Meaux and the anti-Quietist forces depended on a rapid condemnation from the Holy See. Innocent XII, however, proceeded with great deliberation, determined to examine the question with impartiality and thoroughness. He appointed a panel of ten consultors who were to study the controversial propositions of the *Maximes* and report their findings to the cardinals of the Congregation of the Holy Office. To guarantee a favorable decision Bossuet dispatched to the scene his nephew, the Abbé Bossuet, and the Abbé Phélipeaux to act as agents in his behalf. They were instructed to use any means of force and persuasion in a controversy that was all too quickly becoming a game of diplomacy and politics. Fénelon, prohibited from pleading his own cause, sent as his representative his friend the Abbé de Chanterac.

After four months of debate, from September, 1697 to January, 1698, the consultors had reached a stage where a vote was possible. It was, unfortunately, a split decison—five for and five against the *Maximes*. In a move to break the deadlock and reach a positive decision, the Pope appointed two cardinals who were to preside at future sessions. This delay on the part of Rome served only to fan the polemical fires back in France. Up to this time a veritable spate of letters, declarations, responses, and replies had been produced. In June of 1698 Bossuet sprang into action again, publishing his cruel, almost-mocking *Relation sur le quiétisme (Report on Quietism)*. Fénelon's reaction came in the form of a document enti- tled the *Réponse à la Relation de M. de Meaux* (completed before the end of August, 1698). It is Bausset, Fénelon's nineteenth-cen- tury biographer, who credits this *Réponse* with restoring "through a kind of enchantment, happiness and serenity to those who had not ceased to believe in his virtue, and confidence to those who had been weak enough to doubt it" (10, 121). Fénelon's new source of strength only caused Bossuet to redouble his efforts and to urge the king to exert all pressure possible on the Pope.

By the end of the year there was still no decision from the Holy See. Almost as if he were forcing his demands upon Rome, Louis XIV, in January, 1699, dramatically struck Fénelon's name from the list of the royal household; in doing so he deprived him of his pension as preceptor as well as his apartments at Versailles. During this period, too, Fénelon received word that Madame Guyon had died in the Bastille, where she had been confined since June of 1698. He was to learn later that it was an unfounded report; the dead woman in question was the prisoner's attendant. Madame Guyon was, in fact, to be released in 1703 and would survive Féne- lon by some two and a half years.

Finally, in February, 1699, the cardinals of the Holy Office reached a decision. Twenty-three of the thirty-eight propositions from the *Maximes* were judged worthy of censure. It was the Pope's opinion that the decree of condemnation should be in the form of a brief, not a papal bull, and to this suggestion the cardinals agreed. The official document, the *Cum alias*, was signed by Innocent on March 12, 1699. Despite the general rejoicing by Bossuet and his forces, the blow to Fénelon was to some degree softened by the fact that, first of all, the brief carefully avoided the use of the word "heretical" in speaking of the *Maximes* and, secondly, Fénelon's other writings on the subject of mysticism were not condemned. Bossuet had predicted that Fénelon would not submit to Rome's decision; however, when he received the news, on the Feast of the Annunciation, just as he was about to begin his sermon in the cathedral at Cambrai, Fénelon dramatically changed the topic of his sermon. His message to his parishioners became one of submission, of man's obedience to God's will and to the authority of God's representatives on earth. This public statement, as well as his subsequent pastoral letter (April 9) and his letter to the Pope (April 10), stood as Fénelon's manifestation of outward surrender. So far as his "interior submission"[24] was concerned it was another matter entirely. In carefully reading his correspondence, particularly the letter (number III of the series) to Father Le Tellier, written as late as 1710 (7, 665), one can easily agree that "Fénelon never pardoned those who were responsible for his condemnation."[25]

There is a sort of epilogue to this fateful year of 1699, and it concerns not Fénelon's relation to Quietism, but the publication of *Télémaque*. The manuscript of this work, designed, as mentioned earlier, for the education of the Duc de Bourgogne, began to circulate sometime during the last months of 1698. Then, about a month after the condemnation of the *Maximes*, that is, before the end of April, 1699, an anonymous edition containing four and a quarter books was printed in Paris with the following title: *Suite du quatrième livre de l'Odysée, ou les Aventures de Télémaque, fils d'Ulysse (Sequel to the Fourth Book of the Odyssey, or the Adventures of Telemachus, Son of Ulysses)* Judged by many to be a satire on Louis XIV and his regime, the book caused an even greater stir when it was learned that Fénelon was its author. The archbishop maintained that a treacherous copyist had pirated the manuscript and that the *Télémaque* in circulation was an unauthorized edition. The king responded by ordering the confiscation of the work (even though a reported six hundred copies had been sold in a single day,[26] and by dealing Fénelon his final disgrace: not only was the Archbishop of Cambrai never to return to Paris or Versailles, but he was henceforth prohibited from communicating with any member of the royal family.

VII *Fénelon at Cambrai*

The See of Cambrai, located in the northeast region of France, which is still sometimes referred to as Flanders, was composed in part of territory that had been France's for only slightly less than two decades when Fénelon began his permanent residence there in August of 1697. The archbishop's sense of isolation and exile was rendered even more acute by the fact that most of the population of the ten parishes under his jurisdiction was Flemish in language and custom. There is little wonder that most of them were quite openly hostile to their new French prelate. Fénelon's first great task was, therefore, to win the confidence of his flock and to conciliate the differences of nationality and background. In this he was apparently successful by dint of not only his charm, graciousness, and justice, but also through his charity, his parochial visits, and his willingness to preach in city and village church alike. He was assisted in his work by friends of long standing, the Abbé Langeron and the Abbé de Chanterac.

Fénelon's work at Cambrai was made all the more difficult by a turn of events that converted his diocese into a theater of war. In October, 1700, a month before he died, the childless Carlos II of Spain, signed his second will whereby he bequeathed all his territories to Louis XIV's grandson, the seventeen-year-old Philippe, Duc d'Anjou. Louis, hesitant at first, finally decided to reject the two Partition Treaties of 1698 and 1699 and accept the will. Holy Roman Emperor Leopold accordingly urged his former allies, Holland and England, to join in a coalition against France and oppose the claims of the new Philippe V. When French troops occupied the Spanish Netherlands in early February, 1701, conflict seemed inevitable. By April of that year the War of the Spanish Succession had begun, although England did not announce her formal declaration of war until May, 1702.

Fénelon from his own very particular geographical vantage point may have watched the clouds of war roll in, but he did not sit idly by. Long an antiwar partisan, he wished most fervently that France avoid the approaching conflict. To this end he composed, in August, 1701, the first of nine *Mémoires concernant la Guerre de la Succession d'Espagne (Memoirs Concerning the War of the Spanish Succession)* in which he suggested various means of preventing the confrontation. Once he realized that compromise was an impossibility, his thoughts turned to the idea of an honorable victory for France; "He heard the march of the armies and discerned all the moral and material consequences of a battle lost."[27] Then, as early as the autumn of 1706, Fénelon began to focus his attention on the possibilities of peace; and in numerous letters to the Duc de Chevreuse and the Vidame d'Amiens (Chevreuse's son) from 1706 until 1712, he voiced his hopes and plans for negotiations which might end the devastation.

The war machine rumbled on, however, closer and closer to Cambrai. In July, 1708, Marlborough, the British general and

Prince Eugene, Prince of Savoy, defeated the French at Oudenarde, a victory that was followed by the Allies' capture of Lille in October. Next came the severe winter of 1708–1709, when the nightmare of famine replaced for a while the horrors of war. Fénelon, always charitable, strove all the harder to relieve the wretched condition of his parishioners. He even provided wheat from his personal supply for the local garrison. Worse was yet to come, for after the battle of Malplaquet in September, 1709, Cambrai was overrun with wounded soldiers and refugees. Fénelon turned the episcopal palace into a veritable hostel (even the courtyards and gardens serving as an asylum for both man and beast) and the seminary into a hospital for the wounded. Because of his kindness to enemy prisoners of war, it is reported that Fénelon was greatly respected by allied leaders who were in turn considerate of his property.

During this difficult time Fénelon received two visitors of note. The first was the royal exile, James Francis Edward Stuart (1688–1766), sometimes referred to as either the "Old Pretender" or James III of England. While the battle over Mons was raging, James chose the archbishopric palace as a place where he could recuperate from another of his malarial attacks. He also stayed at Cambrai the next year (May, 1710). The second of the visitors was a young Scotsman, Andrew Michael Ramsay, who, drawn to that part of the world by Fénelon's renown, became one of the archbishop's greatest disciples. Not only did Ramsay write the *Histoire de la vie de Fénelon* (*History of the Life of Fénelon, 1723*), the first biography of the prelate, and serve as an important early editor of Fénelon's works, but he also composed the *Essai sur le gouvernement civil* (*Essay on Civil Government*) which is presumably a development of James III's conversations with Fénelon.

Quite a large segment of Fénelon's leisure time at Cambrai was devoted to writings of a philosophical nature. He completed, for example, the *Traité de l'existence et des attributs de Dieu*, (*Treatise on the Existence and Attributes of God*) one part of which he had composed during the 1680s; and in 1713 he began a series of seven letters (three of them addressed to the future regent, the Duc d'Orléans) which in the 1718 edition would bear the title *Lettres sur divers sujets de métaphysique et de religion* (*Letters on Various Metaphysical and Religious Subjects*). To this period belong also his justification for his attitude toward the condemnation of the *Maximes*, as well as the *Lettres sur l'autorité de l'église* (*Letters on*

the Authority of the Church), which discuss certain matters concerning Protestant conversion. Fénelon's greatest energy by far
was, however, expended in his long and concentrated polemic
against Jansenism. It was a heretical doctrine for many Catholics,
since, in matters of predestination and grace, it bore no small resemblance to Calvinism. In 1702, the publication of Father Eu-
stace's *Cas de conscience*, a defense of "respectful silence" on the
subject of the five propositions from the *Augustinus* condemned by
the Pope, had suddenly rekindled the fires of a controversy which
had begun in earnest the decade before Fénelon was born. The
archbishop's active participation in the quarrel, motivated perhaps
to some degree by his desire to ingratiate himself with the Jesuits
and to be forgiven for his part in the Quietist affair, is evidenced by a
stream of pastoral instructions, letters (particularly those to Father
Lamy), *mandements* (episcopal orders and reports) and disserta-
tions. Perhaps the best-known development of his doctrinal objections is the *Instruction pastorale en forme de dialogues (Pastoral
Instruction in the Form of Dialogues)*, published in 1714.

Another very significant part of Fénelon's activity during the
Cambrai years was centered about his continued interest in the Duc
de Bourgogne and the political writings which were a result of that
relationship. Not only did the two resume their correspondence in
1701, but they were able the following year, by royal permission, to
meet (in the presence of witnesses), first in April and again in September. During the disastrous campaign of 1708, while the twenty-
six-year-old Louis was serving in the field under the Duc de Ven-
dôme, Fénelon wrote to him numerous advice-filled letters,
exhorting him, among other things, to correct his irresolution and to
act with courage. Then, approximately three years later, in April,
1711, the Dauphin died. The Duc de Bourgogne was now what
many through the years had suspected he would become, the heir
presumptive to the throne of France. For Fénelon the news was
only the signal for renewed efforts at counseling and instruction. He
had earlier prepared for his former pupil possibly as early as 1697, a
sort of guidebook for rulers in the form of a treatise entitled *Examen
de conscience sur les devoirs de la royauté (Examination of Conscience on the Duties of Royalty)*. Now, he decided, was the time to
draft a less general and more practical manual of kingship. To collaborate on the project Fénelon called in his old friend, the Duc de
Chevreuse, and the two began to formulate their ideas at Chaulnes,

the Picardian estate of the latter's son, during the month of November, 1711.

What dreams Fénelon may have had of seeing his protégé in the role of enlightened monarch, and what ambitions he may have harbored with relation to his own participation in a new regime were suddenly shattered. On February 18, 1712, the Duc de Bourgogne, the heir presumptive to the throne, succumbed to a short (and what was considered at the time a mysterious) illness. Modern diagnosis has decided that it was not poisoning but a fatal case of spotted fever. This bereavement was soon followed by others: in November, 1712, the Duc de Chevreuse died and at the end of August, 1714, the Duc de Beauvillier. Thus at the age of sixty-three Fénelon felt truly old, alone, and disheartened. By the end of 1712 he sensed his health so fragile that he suggested to the Abbé de Beaumont that a *coadjuteur* be assigned to help him with the work of the diocese (7, 483). In a letter written sometime during 1714, he described himself as "only a skeleton who walks and talks, who sleeps and eats but little." The world for him was "full of thorns, troubles, and of odious, deceptive, and dastardly dealings" (8, 541).

Despite Fénelon's deep melancholy and his obvious fatigue, it would be deceptive to color those last few years or so of his life with too somber a hue. One very bright spot in this otherwise gloomy period was his friendship with the Chevalier Destouches (father of D'Alembert, the famous eighteenth-century *philosophe*), which began by way of correspondence in 1711. Fénelon may have reproved him for his gluttony, but he basked in the warmth and cordiality of a man who shared his interests in the classics, particularly Virgil and Horace. Destouches was perhaps more than indirectly responsible for sparking the archbishop's interest in the new phase of the Quarrel of the Ancients and the Moderns, which began in 1713, and for his literary correspondence with (1713–1714) Antoine Houdar de La Motte. This interchange of ideas with both Destouches and La Motte accounts in large part for Fénelon's inspiration to write the last of his works, the *Lettre à l'Académie (Letter to the Academy)*, published in 1716.

In November, 1714, during a pastoral visit, Fénelon's carriage collided with a parapet while crossing a bridge. One of the horses was killed, and the archbishop, although unharmed, reached Cambrai badly shaken. Throughout the following month he continued to perform his duties, but on January 1, 1715, weak and feverish, he took to his bed. Three days later his nephews, the Abbé de Beaumont and the Marquis de Fénelon, arrived from Paris, bringing with them the famous doctor Chirac (10, 324). The latter prescribed what even the most competent of physicians deemed obligatory—a bleeding and an emetic. By January 6, it was obvious that Fénelon could not survive, and he received extreme unction. In the early hours of the following day, he died, seven months before his sixty-fourth birthday and eight months before Louis XIV.

CHAPTER 2

The Early Works

IT is certainly not difficult to accept the conjecture that Fénelon exhibited what certain critics have characterized as a true disdain for literary fame. The fact that, except for the *Traité de l'éducation des filles (Treatise on the Education of Girls)*, the *Traité du ministère des pasteurs (Treatise on the Ministry of Pastors)*, and his writings on Quietism, he never consciously sought to publish his works seems to reinforce the idea of an author who was to a large degree singularly indifferent to public acclaim and critical approval.[1] Fénelon wrote not all, but certainly most of his works to fill the need of a very practical objective which he had in mind. During almost every period in his life he responded to the demands and requirements of circumstances and situations.

In the case of Fénelon's early works, those compositions he produced during the decade that preceded his encounter with Madame Guyon, it was principally the intellectual stimulation of Bossuet and the Germigny group—the "Little Council" as it came to be called—that lay behind his motivation to write. Before his entrance into this erudite sphere of influence, Fénelon, it is assumed, had shown, for example, but scant interest in metaphysics. As a neophyte eager to please Bossuet, he was willing to formulate with the latter's help a refutation of Malebranche, to plunge into a study of Cartesian thought. Also of prime importance was Fénelon's spiritual and ideological affinity with Claude Fleury whom he met in Bossuet's circle and whom he chose later as an associate in the second of the Protestant missions and as his sub-preceptor. Fleury's *Traité du choix de la méthode des études (Treatise on the Choice of Educational Methods)*, which had begun to circulate in manuscript as early as 1675, seems to have profoundly shaped the ideas of the *Traité de l'éducation des filles*. The *Dialogues sur l'éloquence*, too, bear in a

very marked fashion the influence of that wise and learned churchman.[2]

There can be little doubt, then, about the willingness on Fénelon's part to play the role of eager disciple and attentive colleague to
two older and esteemed men. At the same time, however, it would
be misleading to underplay the impact and significance of the practical experience he received in the period immediately following his
departure from Saint-Sulpice. Besides his preaching ministry, there
was the work at Les Nouvelles Catholiques, which not only
broadened his pedagogical views, but also, like his service in the
mission field, brought into sharper focus the problems surrounding
the Protestant question.

I Dialogues sur l'éloquence

As Fénelon reveals in the full title of the work, *Dialogues sur
l'éloquence en général et sur la chaire en particulier (Dialogues on
Eloquence in General and Particularly the Kind Suitable for the
Pulpit)*, his interest in the subject of rhetoric and speech communication goes far beyond the bounds of pulpit oratory alone. It is in the
third and last of the dialogues that his participants, named simply A,
B, and C, turn to a specific consideration of the preacher's needs
and qualifications. Before he chooses to broach that subject, however, Fénelon must introduce his readers, through quiet debate and
discussion, to the problems, complexities, and definitions that have
to do with the work of the secular orator, the poet, and the artist.

The point of departure for the first dialogue is the criticism of an
Ash Wednesday sermon which B has just heard. Somewhat
abruptly, however, with the mention of the word "eloquence"
(defined by B as "the art of speaking well . . . in order to please and
persuade"), the interest of the group shifts to a discussion of the
secular speaker (6, 569). Very quickly A, the chief spokesman of the
interlocutors, the one who, in fact, as Fénelon's mouthpiece orches-
trates and leads the conversation, establishes himself as the partisan
of high moral standards for the speaker. Eloquence in the hands of
the mischievous can only serve to enforce falsehood; and selfish
men, anxious to make a reputation for themselves, become enter-
tainers who extract profit from beautiful but useless words. A then
catalogues the qualities he considers necessary for the speaker: he is
an incorruptible man devoid of passion and self-interest; he leads a
simple life, thereby illustrating what Cicero considered the most

essential of attributes, virtue. Since eloquence and oratory are dedicated to the guidance and improvement of public morals, the orator should be one who can shun financial success. In that way he will have no need to humor anyone, nor will he be tempted by necessity or the dreams of fortune.

In the closing section of the first dialogue, A, once he has elucidated the moral qualities of the orator, directs the colloquy toward an examination of the meaning of true eloquence which is also to include a consideration of the formation of one who would achieve that goal. To underscore his scorn for the pomp of rhetoricians and for the misuse of reason by those who have become, in his opinion, the modern Sophists, A turns to the authority of Plato, actually citing the *Gorgias* and borrowing freely from it. What one needs to combat false speaking, he suggests, is a suitable moral and intellectual preparation. To this end he recommends (and here his concepts rest principally on Plato's *Phaedrus*) the acquisition of not only a general knowledge of man, with particular reference to his interests and his passions, but a particular one as well. This latter study would emphasize a familiarity with the laws, customs, prejudices, and interests dominant in one's age. In effect, the real principles of this training are synonymous with those of the philosopher, for only the latter can assume the role of true orator. A maintains along with Cicero that once rhetoric is separated from philosophy, it is destroyed. Orators then become nothing less than superficial declaimers.

When Fénelon's interlocutors resume their discussion in the second dialogue, they are prepared, now that the moral and intellectual prerequisites of the orator have been established, to deal with the principles and goals which should direct him in the achievement of his art. Since wisdom and knowledge—even dialectical training—alone cannot convince men of goodness, the speaker, so A is convinced, must have other means at his disposal. He must be able to prove, to portray, and to touch ("prouver, peindre, toucher"). Thus eloquence, in terms that are really of Ciceronian inspiration, is reduced to these purposes; and as A states, "Every brilliant thought that does not aim for one of these three things is only a conceit" (6, 581). When A is asked to explain "portraying" (defined by him as the "representation of surrounding features in a lively and sensitive manner so that the listener almost imagines that he sees them"), he is led into a discussion of poetry, its relationship to painting (the former paints for the ears, the latter for the eyes) and its bearing on eloquence (6, 581). Poetry, the "lively depiction of things," although the soul of eloquence, "paints with enthusiasm and with bolder strokes" (6, 581–82). The important consideration at this point is that the speaker and writer should above all portray nature. Conceits ("les jeux de pensées"), puns ("les jeux de mots"), all those expressions serving no substantial purpose and amounting to no more than sparkle, are heartily condemned by A. Likewise, flowery speech, verbal flourishes (which are related to music), and ornamental discourse (which he likens to Gothic architecture) should be shunned by the person who seeks true eloquence. Art that does not hide itself becomes clumsy; eloquence "is only lofty and sublime when she must be" (6, 591).

It is, in fact, Fénelon's concept of the natural that pervades and dominates the whole of this second dialogue. In pausing to consider, for example, the orator's gestures and the effective use of facial expressions, A issues an appeal for the quality of naturalness. If the speaker's words have movement, his body should have the same; if his words are calm and simple, then he should remain motionless. Naturalness is also an important criterion so far as the memorization of a speech is concerned. Too great a preparation, in A's estimation, leads to a loss of negligence, that agreeable absence of artificiality which was characteristic of the most eloquent orators of antiquity.

Fénelon's attack on artificiality also extends to another area of oratory—the question of order and how it should affect the division and arrangement of sermons and speeches. Here he reveals himself, again through the voice of A, as the proponent of a system aimed at combatting the obligatory, arbitrary organization of discourse into a set number (in his time usually three) of divisions or points. Fénelon has A refer to the prevailing method as a "rather modern invention which comes to us from scholastic philosophy" (6, 588). In its stead A proposes an arrangement built on what he calls "a sequence of proofs" (6, 588). Each element is assigned to its own place, the very spot, that is, where it will obtain the desired effect. The first prepares the way for the second, and the second reinforces the first. After stating his premise, the speaker "sets forth the facts in a simple, clear, and sensible manner, emphasizing the circumstances he will use shortly thereafter" (6, 588). He can then draw from the premises and the facts his conclusions. Thus his speech proceeds in a growing fashion and it is not characterized by any clearly designated partitioning.

With the third dialogue Fénelon frees the reader from the spell of the ancient world and the almost overwhelming magnetism of humanism in order to propel him into the realm of Christian eloquence. Plato, Cicero, Longinus, and Dionysius of Halicarnassus—the preferred sources until now—give way to the authority of Saint Paul, Saint Augustine, and Saint Jerome. In the preceding two dialogues the interlocutors' interest in preachers and preaching, although quite evident, has remained for the most part allusive and somewhat incidental. Now they are prepared to discuss the training and resources necessary for the predicator.

The dialogue quickly becomes a paean to not only the church fathers, but particularly to the eloquence of the Scripture. "Even Homer," says A, "never approached the sublimity found in the hymns of Moses . . . Never did a Greek ode attain the grandeur of the Psalms" (6, 596). Isaiah, Jeremiah, Daniel, and Nahum among the prophets merit his special praise as do Matthew, Mark, and Luke, those representatives of the New Testament responsible for revealing the natural grandeur of Christ's preaching. So it is that the sacred orator can borrow without qualms from the Scripture, remembering that its doctrine should be interconnected, and that it should be used as something other than ornament. In this way the preacher can avoid vague and unrelated sermons; he can lead his flock, and systematically so, from the primary elements of religion to the highest mysteries. By following these principles, he does not "stir up applause" (6, 605). He avoids being a declaimer and instead achieves the status of true teacher.

The *Dialogues sur l'éloquence* is to a large extent a document of revolt. It is Fénelon's protest against a prevailing rhetorical style, rigid and inflexible, which his age had inherited principally from the doctrine of Ramus and Talaeus; it is his rejection of their neo-scholastic concept that one must seek as desired expression the unusual and, consequently, the artificial.[3] The *Dialogues* also mirrors Fénelon's low opinion of the pulpit oratory of his day, revealing, for example, his sharp reaction to the set method of arrangement, division, and delivery of sermons. Although he mentions no particular sacred orator by name, he has his characters allude to at least eight contemporary preachers, one of whom (Bourdaloue has been suggested)[4] is given a rather extended critique on the part of A in the second dialogue (6, 584–86).

The *Dialogues sur l'éloquence* has been called "the first modern rhetoric" as well as "the earliest statement we have of what may be said to have become the dominant modern attitude towards rhetoric."[5] At the same time Fénelon's work must also be viewed as a continuation and reinforcement of Antoine Arnauld's *Logique ou l'Art de penser* (*Logic or the Art of Thinking*, 1662) and Bernard Lamy's *De l'Art de parler* (*On the Art of Speaking*, 1675), which Fénelon may not have read; his views on pulpit oratory bear a close resemblance to those found in Joseph Glanvill's *An Essay Concerning Preaching* (1678), which Fénelon in all likelihood did not know.[6] What perhaps may be more significant is the fact that even if the *Dialogues* were written as early as 1678 (Goré and Cherel prefer a later date, probably 1684 or 1685), they were not published until 1718 and therefore exerted no influence on the opinions and theories of Fénelon's era.

Fénelon's adaptation of the basic structure and spirit of the Platonic dialogue is well suited to the aims of this particular work. I quite disagree with the opinion that the *Dialogues* are "long, cold, and monotonous."[7] It is unfortunate that for all their freshness and modernity they have been eclipsed by the better-known *Lettre à l'Académie* (*Letter to the Academy*). It is true enough that the latter work, written some thirty years after the *Dialogues,* is a more extended, more complete development of Fénelon's literary and artistic credo. As the "first expression of his aesthetics,"[8] however, the *Dialogues* deserve to be read as a companion piece to the better-known *Lettre.* They remain the best and most complete expression of his rhetorical theory and a fascinating early revelation of his views concerning the interrelationship of the arts.

II   Sermon pour la fête de l'Epiphanie
(The Epiphany Sermon)

For a long time it was an accepted fact that Fénelon's Epiphany sermon was preached in Paris on January 6, 1685, at the Eglise des Missions Etrangères (The Church of Foreign Missions) in the presence of the Siamese ambassadors. Although this dating has been challenged,[9] the Epiphany sermon (*Sermon pour la fête de l'Epiphanie* or the *Sermon sur la vocation des Gentils,* as it is sometimes called) remains not only a relatively early example of Fénelon's predication, but a typical one as well. Unknown to Fénelon, this sermon was first published in 1706 in a collection entitled *Sermons choisis sur différents sujets* (*Selected Sermons on Different Subjects*).

In the exordium, or introduction, to his Epiphany message,

Fénelon announces the antithetical nature of his sermon in the following manner: "So let us rejoice in the Lord, my brothers, in the Lord who gives glory to his name, but let us rejoice with trembling" (5, 617). It is this duality of emotion, this contrast of sentiment that he seeks to develop and explain in the two divisions which form the body of the sermon.

The first section is a veritable hymn of praise for the missionary zeal of the Church, a song of triumph for the accomplishment of God's promise to form an everlasting kingdom. In a sort of epic tableau, poetic and impassioned, Fénelon traces the evangelization of the world and the growth of Christianity from the early Christian era to his own time. There is special praise for Louis XIV, whom he credits with the aid and encouragement of missions, and a particular tribute to the work of the Jesuits in the Orient. The Bishop of Heliopolis (Pallu, who is mentioned above) also receives a brief encomium for his ministry in Siam, Cochin China, and China. Such achievements, however, do not efface from Fénelon's mind the realization that this work must somehow continue; the faith, simplicity, and joy of former days must be renewed so that the Church, "this city situated atop the mountain," will always be visible (5, 620).

Fénelon's cautionary words here at the end of the first division are carried over to the second section where his thoughts are translated into a jeremiad against the moral decadence and the religious tepidness of his age. Gone are the elements of joy and triumph which he has just celebrated, and in their place he substitutes the "trembling" and the "reprobation" referred to in his introduction. Calling his auditors "fainthearted and unworthy Christians," Fénelon warns them against the evils rampant in their society: pride, ostentation, vanity, love of sensual delights, blasphemy, heresy, impiety, and doubt (5, 623). He does not explain the underlying causes for the degeneration of the Christian ethic (as he will do later in the *Sermon pour la fête de Sainte Thérèse*), although in passing he does refer to the growth of what he calls "instruction," which could well be interpreted to mean science and reason (5, 623). So far as counteractive measures are concerned, the only solution he advances is that all fervent souls should "hold fast to the faith which stands ready to escape us" (5, 624). The prayer that ends the sermon is a petition for the continued prosperity of foreign missions, for the well-being of the universal Church, and for the augmentation of Christian faith.

Although twentieth-century scholar and critic Arthur Tilley finds much of the *Sermon pour la fête de l'Epiphanie* to be "extremely eloquent," he judges that Fénelon in his effort to achieve this quality did not altogether avoid "the pitfalls of exaggeration and bad taste."[10] It may be true that it is marked with certain rhetorical excesses (there is, no doubt, an overuse of apostrophes and prosopopoeia in the first section);[11] but, everything considered, I agree with Marguerite Haillant who in a fairly recent study of the sermons maintains that this example of Fénelon's predication, like all the extant sermons, remains "in perfect accord with the theories that he set forth in his *Dialogues sur l'éloquence.*"[12] Here is certainly a good example of Fénelon the apostolical preacher, far removed from the scholastic tones of a Bourdaloue or a Fléchier, prepared to instruct and move his congregation in a simple, sincere manner. Fénelon's vivid, biblical language may well appeal more to the emotions than to the intellect; that rhetorical quality does not to my mind, however, detract in any way from the vigorous, enthusiastic spirit of this sermon.

III   Traité de l'éducation des filles

Fénelon's treatise on the education of girls, a rather compact work which comprises some thirty-five double-column pages in the Paris edition, was the first of his compositions to be printed. It appeared in March of 1687, but a letter from Fénelon to the Duchesse de Beauvillier, for whom he especially conceived the work, proves conclusively that he had already completed it by late December of 1685.[13]

There is nothing extraordinary or, to say the least, enlightened about Fénelon's view of woman's place in society. He is in fact far removed from the pro-feminist pronouncements of such seventeenth-century figures as Saint Gabriel (*The Merit of Women, Le Mérite des dames,* 1640) and Poulain de la Barre (*On the Education of Women, De l'Education des dames,* 1671). In the opening chapter of the treatise he speaks of her role as most men of his time would have: she has quite simply "a household to manage, a husband to make happy, and children to raise well" (5, 564). Since she is not to enter government service, the army, or the priesthood, there is therefore no need for her to be trained in philosophy, law, theology, military art, or politics—"the more extensive branches of knowledge," as Fénelon describes them (5, 563). This limited sphere of activity does not, however, preclude the girl from developing serious interests; in fact, nothing is more neglected than the education of girls. It is most imperative that they receive an education that will inspire them to virtue and prepare them for fulfilling duties that are "the foundations of all human life" (5, 563). Above all, a girl must not succumb to indolence. To do so means that she will in turn be led to boredom and idle curiosity, at which point she turns her attention toward "vain and dangerous objects" (5, 565). On the other hand, if by chance she should become a bluestocking, reading all manner of books and cultivating a taste for novels, plays, and romantic tales, she faces the great disappointment of having to deal with the workaday world of ordinary people and the routine chores of everyday housekeeping.

Having thus stated the problem, Fénelon is now ready to present the solution. He begins by formulating in chapters III through VIII, which, in effect, form the central section of the treatise, a basic guide for those concerned with the training of boys as well as girls. In stressing the importance of the child's formative period, Fénelon draws attention to not only matters of health and diet, but most particularly to the impressionable, sensitive nature of children. Extremely susceptible to language and body movements, they are therefore inclined to imitate everything they see. Consequently, the best examples must be set; and the brain, that "reservoir which is so tiny and so precious," must be inscribed with the images of "what one hopes will remain there a lifetime" (5, 568).

Chapters V and VI, certainly among the most striking of this middle part of the treatise, serve to define Fénelon's system of "indirect instruction," as he calls it, and to explain how study and instruction can be made attractive and pleasant. Wisdom, he says, must be revealed to the child "gradually and with a smiling face" (6, 569); affectation, pedantry, and harshness on the part of the teacher must be avoided and at no time should the pupil experience fatigue and boredom. Much of this goal he feels can be accomplished through the use of stories—clever and harmless animal fables, appealing tales, and most particularly sacred narratives—designed to make religion "beautiful, agreeable, and majestic" (5, 577). It is also conceivable that children might act out stories, creating little dramas (the story of Isaac and Abraham is suggested as a possibility) which will probably interest them more than other sorts of games. This type of activity will accustom them to think and speak of serious matters in a pleasurable way. The formulation of what might be called Fénelon's pleasure principle is really much more than just a supplement to formal education; as a deterrent to force and restraint and an effective aid in developing the child's natural curiosity, it is intended as an integral part of the educational process.

For the remainder of the treatise (chapters IX through XIII), Fénelon, returning to his announced subject, concentrates exclusively on the education of girls. He begins on a rather negative note, however, with a chapter devoted to their faults. Here there is little which would endear him to modern feminists; proponents of women's liberation would certainly argue that he is guilty of blatant generalizations and of what have come to be called sexist attitudes. For Fénelon, girls, by virtue of their upbringing, are incapable of a "firm and regulated conduct" (5, 587). Passion, not reason, dictates what they say; and it is the former which causes them to talk a great deal. Since they have a pliable nature and maintain besides a high opinion of craftiness, they easily play all sorts of roles. Girls are, moreover, timid and full of false modesty, characteristics which explain in part their use of pretense. Fénelon concludes that they must therefore be shown by examples "how without deceitfulness one can be circumspect, cautious, and diligent in the legitimate means of getting ahead in life. Tell them that the better part of prudence consists in speaking little and of being more distrustful of oneself than of others, but not in making false statements and in sowing discord" (5, 588).

Despite the gravity of the character flaws cited above, Fénelon believes that girls possess an even more serious one: vanity. Finding "the pathways that lead men to important positions and fame" closed to them, they attempt to get ahead in the world through attractiveness of mind and body (5, 588): this compensation on their part explains their inordinate love for dress and their adherence to continued change in fashion—excesses which can produce only disordered mores and the ruination of families. Girls must be made to understand that honor depends on good conduct, and that true ability has nothing to do with one's hair or dress. Fénelon therefore advocates, so far as beauty and adornment are concerned, a return to the natural and the simple, qualities which for him reflect not only the nobility of the ancient world, but also exemplify Christian attitudes of behavior. As in the *Dialogues sur l'éloquence* Fénelon underscores his horror of the artificial and his scorn for the ridiculous; nature, one of the touchstones of Fénelonian aesthetics, stands forth as the trusted guide to good sense, virtue, and worthy aims.

In this last part of the manual Fénelon reminds the reader that he has already mentioned the restrictive aspect of a woman's instruction. What remains for him to do now is to present his observations and suggestions which are related to the fulfillment of the principal vocation open to girls of his time (unless, of course, they entered convents)—that of wife and mother. The education of the children, the supervision of the servants, the management of the household budget and the estate in general should be her responsibilities; and they are tasks that require a certain knowledge. A girl should therefore be taught to read, write, and spell correctly; she is to know the grammar of her native language, "the four rules of arithmetic," and have besides some acquaintance with what Fénelon calls "the chief principles of law" (5, 593–94). She should also be told how to establish schools and charitable organizations, to encourage local industries which might bring relief to the sick and the poor. As for her leisure time, she is encouraged to read: not comedies and novels, but Greek, Roman, and French history. She may learn Latin; but Spanish and Italian, languages "where wit and liveliness of imagination hold sway in unbridled fashion," are not to be part of her curriculum (5, 595). Poetry and music are suitable, provided they do not tend to overexcite the mind. Above all, the education of a girl should prepare her for her social milieu and the work that is most likely to occupy her.

It would be unwise either to exaggerate the originality of Fénelon's ideas on education or to deemphasize the significance of his innovations in pedogogical theory. He was certainly not the first to be concerned with female education. Xenephon, for example, in the *Oeconomicus* offered advice on the training of daughters. In the early Christian era, Saint Jerome, in his letters to Laeta and Gaudentius, had accomplished exactly what Fénelon does in his treatise. During the Middle Ages there was a concern for women's rights and a desire to improve their educational status, a trend that was renewed through the work of such Renaissance thinkers as Vives and Erasmus. As for the matter of an "attractive," agreeable education, Fénelon's methods reflect much of the same spirit that is to be found not only in Montaigne, but in the theory of two seventeenth-century pedagogues, Ratich (1571–1635) and Comenius (1592–1670).[14]

It is difficult, nonetheless, not to think of Fénelon as a pioneer; and I quite agree with the concept that, even though we may find the pages of the treatise obvious and platitudinous, "We forget its astonishing novelty to a society in which education, where it was attempted at all, consisted in cramming into boys and girls with the aid of a cane, a number of unexplained and disconnected facts."[15] In this respect, Fénelon bridges the gap, so far as French traditions in education are concerned, between François Rabelais (1494?–c. 1553), who, it must be admitted, was interested only in educating boys, and Jean-Jacques Rousseau (1712–78). The *Traité de l'éducation des filles,* with its plea "to follow and aid nature," its emphasis on the value of utilizing concrete objects and avoiding the abstract, also anticipates the work of educationists such as Pestalozzi (1746–1827) and Friedrich Froebel (1782–1852). Most of all, it stands as proof that there did exist a pre-Enlightenment "cult for the child";[16] that Fénelon, along with Madame de Maintenon, was an important precursor in the effort to free children from a stale, artificial, and claustral atmosphere where the pleasures and natural activity of childhood were preempted in favor of the demands and interests of an adult society.

We must be careful to remember, however, that the freedom and confidence exhibited in the *Traité* have their boundaries. The "unconstrained and easy" atmosphere which Lemaître finds in this work is, as a matter of fact, held very strictly within the confines of the Christian ethic. It is quite debatable whether Fénelon, as Lemaître contends, speaks more as an *honnête homme* (a refined and cultured gentleman) than he does as an *homme d'église* (a man of the cloth).[17] A very large part of the work is devoted to the problems of religious instruction, and Fénelon's Christian aims more than obviously explain his mistrust of the comedy and the novel, not to speak of his unreceptive, rather cautious attitude toward music. Unlike Jean-Jacques Rousseau, he does not believe that the goal of education is to make the student happy. This epicurean attitude is basically foreign to Fénelon, although his system lends itself to such an interpretation. It would perhaps be more valid to accept the *Traité de l'éducation des filles* as an offshoot of the tradition of the Christianized Renaissance, a work which is imbued with the positive spirit of the Abbé Fleury and with certain traces of Fénelon's latent mysticism.[18]

IV   Réfutation du système du Père Malebranche sur la nature et la grâce *(Refutation of the System of Father Malebranche Concerning Nature and Grace)*

Nicolas Malebranche, the scholarly and ascetic Oratorian priest, presented a somewhat curious, disturbing image to many of his contemporaries. Here was a man who in unabashed fashion reconciled his commitment to science and reason with his deep religious faith. A disciple of both Descartes and Saint Augustine, Malebranche revealed himself to be not only a strikingly original philosopher-theologian, but a revolutionary one as well. From the time of his first published work, *De la Recherche de la vérité (Concerning the Search for Truth*, 1674–75), until his death in 1715, he was a central figure in polemical frays involving many philosophers from a variety of schools.

Bossuet, the self-appointed paladin, the ever-present watchdog of the true church, became an active opponent of Malebranche soon after the publication of the latter's *Traité de la nature et la grâce (Treatise on Nature and Grace)* in 1670. Although Bossuet knew that Antoine Arnauld, the well-known Jansenist, was preparing a reply to Malebranche's bold, unorthodox views, he encouraged Fénelon to try his hand at a refutation. The project, begun probably around 1684 under the watchful eye of his mentor (the corrections to the manuscript are in Bossuet's handwriting), was completed more than likely in 1687. Fragments of the work were published in 1717 in *Les Nouvelles littéraires*, but, for reasons that are still unexplained, the complete text of the *Réfutation du système du Père Malebranche sur la nature et la grâce (Refutation of the System of Father Malebranche on Nature and Grace)* was not published until 1820, when it appeared in volume three of the Versailles edition.[19]

Fénelon's refutation is a long (thirty-six chapters covering eighty-five double-column pages in the Paris edition) and laborious effort to counteract a system that he believed was philosophically interesting but theologically unsound. For one thing, Malebranche's view of universal order, in Fénelon's estimation, seriously limits God's freedom. According to the Oratorian, God, being an infinitely perfect Being, can produce nothing which does not bear the stamp of His infinite perfection. Thus, His wisdom determines Him to produce the most perfect of works. Fénelon counters by saying that God never chooses the most perfect, "for He chooses only among possible plans, and all possible plans are equally perfect" . . . (2, 77). If in creating the world, for example, God performed a more perfect act than in not creating it, how does one explain that a temporal creation is less perfect than an eternal one?

This alarming sort of fatalism or determinism was attacked in another way by Fénelon through his objection to Malebranche's belief in a "simplicité de voies" (a simplicity of means), a concept which holds that no degree of perfection can be added to God's work, since He produces the most perfect work He can in general ways. God thus chooses to act with the least number of "volontés particulières" (special wills or interventions), even at the expense of allowing in many instances the presence of injustice and grief. Fénelon cannot accept this optimistic theory of total perfection; and, to prove his point, refers as one example to the creation of the world: "If God had limited himself to the general laws of movement, in one instant all the bodies of the universe would have been set in movement in order to put each one in its place. But the vast extent of the universe would have made this arrangement impossible in six days" (2, 97). What Fénelon visualizes basically is an infinitely superior being completely free to choose; God's perfection is found not in the work, but in the creative act.

The other major points of the refutation deal with the questions of free will and grace. Fénelon, like others, finds that Malebranche's concept of grace, which is difficult to separate from his theory concerning providence, fluctuates between Pelagianism (man in complete control of his fate) and Jansenism (man controlled by predestination). He refuses to accept the excursion of Malebranche the philosopher into the realm of the spiritual. Relying mainly on the tenets of Saint Augustine, Fénelon prefers to see human will as dependent on God, but at the same time free and uncompromised. Our liberty itself is, in fact, the product of grace: it is through God and in God that we are free and that we become deserving of His grace.

To all indications, Fénelon never revised his opinion about Malebranche's theory of grace. However, almost from the beginning, a certain fraternity of spirit bound the two men together. Gradually, in an evolutionary fashion that would be difficult to trace, Fénelon would come to think of metaphysical problems in much the same way as Malebranche. Both men, "airy, ethereal," lend to philosophical speculation a blend of mysticism and Cartesian thought.[20] For both of them, it is God's simple and infinite light which illuminates man's mind, affording him a vision otherwise impossible to secure.

Only a scattered number of readers, I suspect, would agree with Sainte-Beuve that Fénelon's refutation of Malebranche "is perhaps his best philosophical work."[21] Even the "pure" language and the dialectical power do not compensate for the basic uninviting quality of this composition.[22] The general, nonspecialized reader is very apt to concur with Crouslé's judgment that "a large part of the book is terribly thorny and hard to follow."[23] The *Réfutation du système du Père Malebranche* is, in fact, probably the least read of the early works. It deserves, however, more than just a fleeting attention; for it is an early proof of Fénelon's intellectual powers and an interesting prelude to the later *Lettres sur divers sujets de métaphysique et religion* and the *Traité de l'existence de Dieu*. The *Réfutation* serves, moreover, as a type of training ground for the Quietist battle in which the author will demonstrate with greater amplitude his talent and virtuosity as a polemicist.

V Traité du ministère des pasteurs
(Treatise on the Ministry of Pastors)

Although most of Fénelon's work in the area of Protestant conversion centered about his very practical duties as counselor and preacher, he did decide, probably sometime between 1685 and 1686, to write a treatise that would define in a more formal way his view of Catholic authority. The result was the *Traité du ministère des pasteurs (Treatise on the Ministry of Pastors)* published in August of 1688.

Fénelon limits his treatise to a defense of one particular principle: the doctrine of apostolic succession, a tenet of the Church which holds that the ministry created by Christ, and originating with the disciples, has been passed in an unbroken chain from century to century. For Fénelon, the Protestant ministry, because of this inviolable and irrevocable succession, is not a legitimate one; in fact, he considers the whole of the reform movement nothing more than a "usurpation of the ministry and a revolt of the people against their pastors" (1, 150). The Protestants, according to Fénelon, have erred in assuming that (1) the people possess a "natural" right to choose through popular election the pastor who acts as the mediator between heaven and earth, and that (2) ordination, or the laying on of hands, is a simple, exterior ceremony, instituted by humans, devoid of any sacramental quality. To refute these claims, Fénelon calls upon the authority of the Scripture, particularly the observations of Saint Paul concerning the ministry as seen in Ephesians, I and II Timothy, and Titus. He also demonstrates how the Protestants have indulged in a too literal interpretation of Tertulian and Saint Augustine in order to prove their claims to any sort of rightful succession. Fénelon also finds that, in certain instances, they have not read their doctrinal sources thoroughly enough and, to illustrate this point, he cites their shallow knowledge of Saint Cyprian.

The *Traité du ministère des pasteurs* presents as one of its more dominant overtones the affirmation of the author's belief that the Church is in no way a political unit in which civil laws hold sway; instead, he likens it to "a kingdom where everything is grace and mercy" (1, 154). Fénelon emphasized the eternal quality of the Church, reminding the Protestants that the true edifice will not fall in ruin and desolation. The conception of which they speak has never been predicted, at least certainly not by the Scripture. In the prayer that ends his treatise he voices a plea for Christian unity; his fervent wish is that the "flocks wandering and dispersed upon all the mountain sides" will listen to the voice of true pastors, that they will return to form "one single flock, a single heart, and a single soul" (1, 202).

It is important to remember that the doctrine examined and defended by Fénelon in the *Traité du ministère des pasteurs* had already been confirmed by Bossuet in certain of his polemical writings against the Protestants, the *Réfutation du catéchisme du sieur Ferry*, for example, which appeared in 1654. While reminding us of this fact, scholars such as Cagnac and Lemaître also call attention to a very salient feature of Fénelon's treatise: whereas Bossuet destined his work for the more learned reader, Fénelon (who very well may have been writing principally for the edification of the young ladies of Les Nouvelles Catholiques) purposely refrained from infusing his explanations with "too much theology."[24] Concentrating on making his interpretation more accessible to "less cultivated minds,"[25] he succeeded in creating a work that is indeed thoroughly readable. Although it is marked with a slightly repetitious quality (chapter IX, for example, echoes much of what can be found in the opening chapters), the *Traité du ministère des pasteurs*, for the most part, possesses the same clarity and fluidity evident in the *Dialogues sur l'éloquence* and the *Traité de l'éducation des filles*.

VI Sermon pour la profession religieuse d'une nouvelle convertie

Fénelon's *Sermon pour la profession religieuse d'une nouvelle convertie (Sermon for the Act of Profession of a New Convert)*, another surviving example of his predication which dates from the period under consideration, forms an interesting parallel to the treatise discussed above. Although the date for this sermon and the circumstances surrounding its delivery are uncertain, it serves to increase our knowledge of Fénelon's work in the field of Protestant missions. For a long while it was believed that this message was given at Saint-Cyr in January, 1687, as part of the ceremony for the act of profession of Geneviève de Montfort.[26] A new theory suggests, however, that it was pronounced on the occasion of the investiture of Guichard de Peray (Sister Charlotte de Saint-Cyprien) on May 12, 1688, a year and a day before she took the veil as a Carmelite nun. The young lady in question, it would seem, had been brought to Les Nouvelles Catholiques in March, 1686, where she fell under the influence of Fénelon who was instrumental in her conversion to Catholicism.[27]

The printed text of this particular sermon reveals no formal division, but the two distinct sections into which Fénelon divides his other sermons are evident in its arrangement. The first of these deals with Fénelon's theory of "the psychology of the heretic."[28] It is his attempt to explain the underlying motive for the Protestant's resistance to conversion. To Fénelon's mind the great barrier to the surrender of the soul is pride. And it is this pride which "misuses the first-fruits of reason," turning "God's greatest gifts against God himself" (5, 655). Even Protestants who receive the sacraments of their reformed church remain Catholic, Fénelon claims, up until the time they exert their reason ("a weak reason which believes itself strong") in order to question the infallibility of the true church (5, 655). What is the answer to this evil? Can it be the Scripture? Fénelon arrives at an answer in the following manner: the Protestants recognize that the Scripture is incomprehensible without grace; and since grace is given only to the humble, it follows that one must be humble to understand it. The Protestants, "so great in their own eyes," cannot, however, because of the exertion of their pride, be considered humble (5, 656). They are incapable, therefore, by their own admission, of comprehending the Scripture. They are walled in, moreover, by a prejudice that refuses any examination of their faith; their religion rests not on the word of God, but on their pride. Humility alone can lead them back to unity and to authority.

Leaving behind the question of pride and humility, Fénelon in the second section concentrates on refuting some of the more common Protestant objections to Catholic doctrine and practice. To lend what he may very well have considered a dramatic flair to the occasion, he places his arguments in the mouth of the new convert; it is she who must now step forward to speak to her errant people. She must defend, for example, the real presence of Christ in the eucharist: "So far as God's gifts are concerned, everything is real . . . This flesh which in a real way His son assumed for all men in general . . . He gives to each of us in particular in the eucharist with the same reality" (5, 658); the cult for images: "I honor the image [of Christ on the cross] as I do the Gospels, which are also an image of the actions and words of the Savior" (5, 569); and the liturgy in Latin: "Is Latin more unknown to the Christian peoples than French of the past century is to the peasants of Gascony and of so many other provinces . . ." (5, 569). These justifications are, as it were, the product of the humble spirit of the young novice. Beneath it all, however, we hear words that are controlled by the persuasive, emotional voice of Fénelon.

As in the *Traité du ministère des pasteurs*, Fénelon's invalidation of Protestant claims is carried out with a basic simplicity. The method employed in both the treatise and the sermon is also, as Haillant concludes, essentially the same: it is a technique of "despoilment," a stripping away of authority and pride, a process whereby the recalcitrant soul is subjected to a view of the crumbling foundations of his faith.[29] There is an almost razor-sharp incisiveness present in Fénelon's message, but it emerges nonetheless as an evangelical lesson in Christian love and unity. Although his activity in the late 1680s is characterized to a large degree by his polemical writings against the Protestants, his concern for Catholic solidarity will never completely fade from sight. Later, during the Cambrai years, in both the *Lettres sur divers sujets de métaphysique et de religion* and the *Lettres sur l'autorité de l'église* he will continue to strike out against the dangers of a doctrine that he regarded as nothing short of heretical.

CHAPTER 3

An "Attractive Education: The Fables and the Dialogues des morts

I The Fables

FOR the seventeenth century the word *fable* was often used to designate not only the animal apologue of Aesopian origin, but plot, story, or narrative in general. The broad sense of the term applies to Fénelon's *Fables*, for these instructive prose narratives, intended specifically for his royal pupil, are an assortment of fairy tales, animal fables, mythological stories, and pastoral and adventure romances. It is impossible to know exactly when Fénelon either began or completed this collection of thirty-six stories. What is conceivable, however, is that this first venture of his in the area of imaginative literature began as early as 1690. Twenty-five of the *Fables* first appeared as something of an addendum to the 1718 edition of the *Dialogues des morts (Dialogues of the Dead)*.

A. *The Fairy Tales*

Fénelon was aware, as others before and since his time, that the fairy tale was a very effective medium for stimulating the child's imagination while at the same time serving as a major element of his socialization.[1] Seven of the stories in the collection therefore rely on elements of the marvellous for their depiction of a universe where superhuman creatures intervene in the affairs of ordinary men to direct them toward either an achievement of happiness or a realization that fame and worldly goods do not constitute the true meaning of life.

Three of the tales from this particular group, "Histoire d'une

53

vieille reine et d'une jeune paysanne" ("Story of an Old Queen and a Young Peasant Girl," I), "Histoire de la Reine Gisèle et de la Fée Corysante ("Story of Queen Gisela and the Fairy Corysante," II), and "Histoire de Florise" ("The Story of Florise," IV), recount how peasant maidens are changed into queens and princesses. In each instance the transformation from rural simplicity to royal grandeur brings with it in one fashion or another unhappiness (or, in the case of Florise, a narrow escape from death). Neither Péronnelle, Corysante, nor Florise can adjust to the disenchantments of life among the mighty; "chagrin," "grief," "misfortune" are the most frequent words that Fénelon uses to describe a life filled with complications and devoid of simple pleasures. Each of the girls is eventually restored to her original milieu, convinced that riches and social position do not ensure contentment and tranquility. Fénelon's glorification of the unspoiled life in a rustic setting, somewhat understated in this group of stories, will reappear in more explicit terms in the pastoral stories as well as later in *Télémaque*.

The "Histoire d'une jeune princesse" ("Story of a Young Princess," III) represents Fénelon's one departure in the collection from the didactic and the moral. This tale is about a princess (unnamed) who, in order to be saved from marriage to an eighteen-foot ogre, is turned into a linnet by a friendly fairy. This clever disguise is not, however, entirely satisfactory, for the monster threatens to eat the king and his court unless he can produce his daughter. The dilemma is resolved by the arrival of Prince Aglaor, a completely charming young man except for the fact that he has eleven mouths (the standard one plus one at the end of each of his fingers). He fights the giant, kills him, and thus wins the hand of the princess (now reconverted to her original form) in marriage. Much more than in the other fairy tales, Fénelon emphasizes here the fantastic and the unusual. Perhaps because it concentrates solely on entertainment, this tale gives the impression of being less contrived than the other *Fables*. Written in the tradition of the popular tale, it is also the one story by Fénelon which is reminiscent of Charles Perrault, the best-known author of fairy tales in the seventeenth century.[2]

Closely related in theme and plot, the three remaining fairy tales employ the enchanted-ring motif to explore the dangers of power and prosperity for those who have tenuous moral values. The first of these, "Histoire du Roi Alfaroute et de Clariphile" ("Story of King Alfaroute and Clariphile," V) relates how a ruler uses a fairy's gifts, a ring which has the property of rendering him invisible and eagle-like wings that are capable of transporting him great distances in a short time, to further his ambitions for power and authority. As Alfaroute's might increases, so do his suspicions concerning his fellow man. His cynicism and mistrust lead him to the tragic mistake of spying on his own wife, Clariphile. One day the latter receives a secret visit from the aforementioned fairy, who must now appear at court disguised as a soldier since she is *persona non grata* for having warned the king about the fatal consequences of the magical wings. When the two friends embrace, Alfaroute, obviously believing the worst, runs Clariphile through with his sword.

The "Histoire de Rosimond et de Braminte" ("Story of Rosimond and Braminte," VI), is the story of two brothers, one virtuous (Rosimond) and the other evil (Braminte), and their reactions to newly acquired power. Whereas Rosimond uses his magic ring (which, like Alfaroute's, renders him invisible) to effect the happiness and well-being of others, his brother employs the talisman for purposes of treachery and deceit. Fénelon carries the contrast even further by having Rosimond, on the verge of possessing great wealth, renounce his princely life and return to his former home where he can till the soil. Braminte, who represents Fénelon's maxim that "prosperity is the source of all evil for the wicked," pursues a life of crime until his villainy is exposed and he is executed (6, 203).

"L'Anneau de Gygès" ("Gyges' Ring," VII), the last of the fairy tales, is still another object lesson on the baleful effects of worldly success and material gain. While tending his flocks, Callimaque, the protagonist of this narrative, finds in a cave a magic ring which once belonged to a Lydian shepherd, Gygès. Belonging very much to the same race of men as Alfaroute, he reaches the pinnacle of fame, wealth, and respect only to find that he lacks the greatest possessions—peace and happiness. The last image we have of him is that of a lost and wandering soul, a sort of romantic hero, who has not learned that "when through opulence and grandeur one loses simplicity, innocence, and moderation, then one's heart and conscience, which are the true seats of happiness, become the prey of trouble, worry, shame, and remorse" (6, 206).

Unlike the other fairy tales, this story attempts to transport the reader to a definite historical period. Thus Fénelon introduces as secondary characters Croesus, the fabled Lydian king, and his

enemy Cyrus the Persian, at whose courts most of the action tran-
spires. Through the creation of the villain Orodes, who is capable of
invoking the aid of Hecate and the Furies, Fénelon also gives this
tale a mythological aura. Finally, more than the other stories of this
category, "L'Anneau de Gygès" relies for its effect on descriptive
passages. The evocation of the exotic splendor of Croesus' palace
and gardens, for example, serves not only as an element of visual
stimulation, but as a stern reminder to his young prince that the
taste for sumptuous buildings is not a desirable one.[3]

B. "Voyage dans L'Ile des Plaisirs" ("Voyage to Pleasure Island")

This particular tale, by dint of its subject and manner of treatment, merits its own special category. Part imaginary voyage, part
dream fantasy, the "Voyage dans L'Ile des Plaisirs" ("Voyage to
Pleasure Island," VIII) recounts the gustatory, olfactory, and visual
experiences of an unnamed traveler as he visits two extraordinary
islands and a most unusual city. Enclosed in this bit of pleasurable
fiction is Fénelon's indictment against gluttony and his warning
against man's surrender to the temptation of sensual delights.

The story, told in the first person, begins with the narrator's
discovery of a land mass composed of sugar; here the mountains are
stewed fruit, the rock formations caramel, the rivers syrup, and the
forests licorice. The voyager does not linger in this paradise, but
journeys on to another island which offers food of a more substantial
variety—mines of ham, sausage, and stew; brooks of onion sauce,
and red wine which falls in the place of rain. This kingdom of highly
seasoned delights is inhabited by two types of tradesmen, the appe-
tite vendors and the dream merchants. The narrator buys a portion
of dreams; he is, however unable to fall asleep, for he is driven from
his bed by an earthquake (a nightly occurrence, moreover), which
causes the lower regions to vomit forth boiling streams of chocolate
mousse and all sorts of liqueurs. He partakes of these offerings and
promptly falls asleep. After dreaming of a realm where the inhabitants are fed on perfumes, the narrator himself experiences the
phenomenon of being nourished only on wonderful odors: for lun-
cheon he chooses orange blossom; for dinner tuberoses, and for
supper a medley of sweet-smelling flowers and burning perfumes.
Later that evening, he finds that he has indigestion, caused, as he
says, "by having smelled too many nourishing odors" (6, 207).

In the closing section, the traveler, borne aloft in a sort of sedan chair pulled by four ostrich-like birds, flies to a marble city, described as being three times larger than Paris. Despite the fact that here all people are equal and therefore in no way aware of class distinctions, they are catered to by "Wishes," lively little spirits that flit about granting each person's desires instantly. The storyteller is treated to a concert of perfumes, or as he calls it, "a harmony which tickles the sense of smell" (6, 208). He finds time to comment on the local mores—strange ones, indeed, since the men perform domestic chores and the women occupy the positions of judges, teachers, and soldiers. This reversal of roles, which is reminiscent of the Torelore episode in *Aucassin et Nicolette*, has come about because the men, served so well by the "Wishes," have become indolent and faint-hearted. Deeply affected by this situation, the narrator, before departing, feels constrained to admit that "sensual pleasures, no matter how varied or readily available, are degrading and do not make one happy" (6, 208).

In his recent study of the French story of fantasy and marvels (1690–1790), Jacques Barchilon cites the "Voyage dans L'Ile des Plaisirs" as an example to support his opinion that the *Fables* exhibit what he terms "contradictory characteristics." He finds that Fénelon possesses a "marvellous" and "exuberant" imagination, but that his talent is to some degree dulled by an overabundance of details and adjectives; that in the end the reader is rebuffed by the moral, didactic quality which is all too obvious.[4] Barchilon's choice of this story to illustrate his point is, to my mind, a poor one. I find the "Voyage" Fénelon's most captivating, most original illustration of his concept of indirect instruction. The synaesthesial effects, which in a way anticipate what we will experience in the works of, for example, Charles Baudelaire and J.-K. Huysmans; the inventive fun, which we tend to associate with latter-day children's stories, contribute to making this fable an innovative and memorable creation.

C. *The Animal Fables*

Unlike the fables of Jean de La Fontaine (1621–95), which are not concerned primarily with practical instruction, and which in many instances accord only a secondary place to any sort of moral, Fénelon's animal apologues are incisively didactic and indisputably pedagogical. Most of the sixteen fables of this group, rather spare, concise compositions of from one to two pages, contain a moral tag and therefore leave virtually no room for any speculation about their intent. The lessons to be taught are expressed in a variety of themes ranging from the necessity for patience ("La Patience et l'éducation corrigent bien des défauts," "Patience and Education Correct Many Defects," IX) and the disadvantages of anger and cruelty ("L'Abeille et la mouche," "The Bee and the Fly," XI), to the dangerous effects of curiosity ("Le Renard puni de sa curiosité," "Curiosity Punishes the Fox," XII) and flattery ("Le Loup et le jeune mouton," "The Wolf and the Lamb," XV).

Three of the animal fables, less general than the above, deserve special attention, mainly because they have a specific political bearing: "L'Assemblée des animaux pour choisir un roi" ("The Assembly of Animals Chooses a King," XXVIII) is a caution against cruelty and vanity and an endorsement of strength and wisdom as those qualities necessary for a ruler while "Les Deux Lionceaux" ("The Two Lion Cubs," XXIX) praises the salutary effects of a spartan life and condemns the soft and idle life of a courtier. Finally, there is "Les Abeilles" ("The Bees," XXX), the most politically oriented of all, since it not only glorifies work, order, and merit, but elucidates in specific terms those duties requisite to a good and vigilant sovereign—the protection of his people and a concern for all phases of their welfare.

Not all the threads of this inherent didacticism, however, are woven into a dull and overbearing fabric of ungracious teaching. The tedium of an incessant moral tone is on occasion relieved by flashes of verve. This quality is perhaps best represented by "Le Singe" ("The Monkey," XVIII), a fable about a monkey who returns from Hades reincarnated as a parrot. Bought by an old lady, who spoils him, he plays his role to perfection until, as Fénelon puts it, "He fretted and fumed so much in his cage and drank so much wine with the old lady that he died" (6, 212). The moral of the fable comes later, after he returns to earth a second time as a boring, loud-mouthed human: "O how many men you find in this world with affected gestures, a bit of idle chatter, and a capable air about them, who have neither sense nor good behavior" (6, 212)! For a moment, at any rate, before the moral engulfs the tale, the image of the monkey-parrot tippling with his mistress affords the reader a glimpse of Fénelon's imaginative, animated spirit.

For the adult reader Fénelon's animal fables lack, then, not vivacity, but rather a certain detachment and sophistication. They do not have that "rich blend of sympathy, tenderness, and irony" which has been attributed to the creations of La Fontaine.[5] Fénelon, here as elsewhere in the *Fables*, is more the moralizer than the moralist; rarely does he desert the educative goal that he has in view, with the result that his universe is one of restricted emotions and carefully controlled behavior.

D. *The Pastoral Mood*

The collection includes three rather brief (no more than three or so pages each) prose idylls and two longer (some seven to eight pages) narratives which serve as Fénelon's evocation of a Virgilian world of rustic beauty and arcadian serenity. Each of the stories is, however, more than just a stylized reconstruction of a pastoral landscape, replete with a variety of descriptive phrases and a goodly number of conventional pastoral images; like practically all the *Fables*, they demonstrate the author's unmistakable didactic interest.

The first of the idylls, "Le Rossignol et la fauvette" ("The Nightingale and the Warbler," XXIV), is really nothing more than Fénelon's poetic means of revealing his dreams and aspirations for his young charge. In a sacred grove frequented by nymphs, fauns, and the three Graces, the nightingale Philomela and a young warbler espy a shepherd whom they first take to be Apollo. Because of his gracious and noble mien, they are inspired to express in song all their wishes for those qualities that they hope one day he will possess: wisdom, virtue, courage, moderation, and charity. These woodland creatures thus become Fénelon's agents of indirect instruction, communicating in a devious but attractive manner feelings that if expressed in a different form or manner might have seemed either slightly obsequious or a little exaggerated.

The second example of Fénelon's pastoral mood is "Le Départ de Lycon" ("Lycon's Departure," XXV), which reiterates (here in more extended fashion than in the fairy tales) his allegiance to the idea that the force of nature, in its guileless and uncomplicated manner, will in the end triumph over ostentation and disordered pleasure. Man, Fénelon is saying, once he knows the joys of the pastoral life, will ultimately return to the place where the voice of nature speaks of harmony, peace, and fruitfulness.

The third of the idylls, "Le Berger Cléobule et la nymphe Phidile" ("The Shepherd Cléobule and the Nymph Phidile," XXXIV), is composed principally of a song which a shepherd offers to his beloved to convince her of his devotion. Cléobule, recently returned from having served Polynices in his campaign against Thebes, sings of his military exploits, describing for Phidile a battle in which he slays a Theban. From a tower the dying man is watched by his wife who is "pierced by an inconsolable grief." Cléobule admits that he would willingly die if he could be so loved. What good is valor and glory, he maintains, if one cannot move the object of his desires. Phidile, won over by his recitation, agrees to marry him. This narrative is a rather subtle blending of a battlefield episode (anticipatory of the ones in Books II, XIII, and XV of *Télé-maque*), designed to appeal to a young reader, and pastoral scenes which once more extol the innocence and joy of rustic life.

In the next of the pastoral stories, "Histoire d'Alibée, persan" ("The Story of Alibée the Persian," XXXIII), we see a protagonist who is closely akin to Rosimond. Alibée, a young shepherd, is discovered by King Schah-Abbas while the latter is travelling about the country observing his people "in all their natural freedom" (6, 223). Impressed by Alibée's bearing and temperament, the king takes him back to his court, educates him, and eventually elevates him to a position of great trust. Everything goes well for Alibée until Schah-Abbas dies and his son succeeds him. Prompted by cour-tiers jealous of Alibée's success, the new king investigates the former royal favorite's handling of the treasury. A carefully locked room, which Alibée's enemies are sure contains the ultimate proof of his thievery and embezzlement, turns out to be the depository—a sort of shrine, as it were—of nothing more than his shepherd's crook, his flute, and his rustic clothes. These remnants of his former life have served as the reminders of an innocent and simple existence; at the end of the story, long after his probity has been reestablished, Alibée still has his accoutrements at hand, ready to reclaim them should "inconstant fortune" lead him again to disfavor.

Fénelon's "Alibée" owes, no doubt, an unmistakable debt to La Fontaine's fable "Le Berger et le roi ("The Shepherd and the King") But, as has been pointed out, there is a decided difference between the two treatments: whereas La Fontaine's shepherd is a worldly, prudent courtier who knows how to renounce grandeur once it begins to grow dangerous, Fénelon's hero teaches us that "true virtue consists of not only scorning honors and wealth, but what is much more difficult, of remaining humble and modest in the very midst of these honors and riches."[6]

In the fifth and final pastoral story, "Les Aventures de Mélésichthon" ("The Adventures of Mélésichthon," XXXV), Fénelon creates the most complete tableau of the idealized pastoral life that we shall see before encountering the utopian marvels of Baetica (La Bétique) in Book VII of *Télemaque*. Mélésichthon is a warrior ruined by expenses incurred during his campaigns. He retires with his wife Proxinée to the country, but the solitude of his new home does nothing to alleviate his feelings of misfortune and unhappiness. The goddess Ceres appears to him in a dream, explaining the way to virtue and contentment: he must adopt the "hard-working" life in order to earn that small degree of this earth's goods (6, 226). Mélésichthon proceeds to follow the goddess's instructions with the result that the living that he procures for his family, although simple and devoid of luxurious display, is abundant.

Fénelon's portrait of a primitivistic society, even for some present-day back-to-nature adherents, is, I suspect, much too overdrawn and far too artificial. The reader is certainly inclined to agree that Mélésichthon's land of plenty, where everything is vibrant and serene, is the author's "pagan dream," in no way meant to be a realistic picture of rural life.[7] This fable, like many others in the collection, is in essence Fénelon's means, forced though it may be, of disabusing the young prince of the sumptuous, corrupt, and idle life at court. This nostalgic, backward glance at a golden age stands as his metaphor for a life of service and virtue.

E. *The Mythological Tales*

Five of the *Fables* utilize mythological personages as characters who are central or near-central to the action of the story. Of this number, two are interesting in that they contain more than obvious allusions to the Duc de Bourgogne. In "Le Jeune Bacchus et le faune" ("Young Bacchus and the Faun," XXI), Fénelon is apparently reminding his pupil that he should be more patient about his teacher's corrections, that even a king's son is capable of committing errors. "Aristée et Virgile" ("Aristeas and Virgil" XXIII) tells of that Roman poet's visit to the underworld where, guided about by Aristeas, he encounters, among others, Homer, Hesiod, and Orpheus, for whom he agrees to recite his verses. His performance, exceptionally well received, ends with Hesiod's prediction that one day a child will translate Virgil's poetry, and that he will share with him "the honor of having sung about the bees" (6, 215). While written as a tribute to the author of the *Aeneid*, this tale is also quite possibly, as Lemaître suggests, Fénelon's reward to the young nobleman for having prepared a good translation of Virgil's *Georgics*.[8]

The best developed of the mythological tales, certainly from the standpoint of theme and characterization, is the "Prière indiscrète de Nélée, petit-fils de Nestor" ("The Imprudent Prayer of Neleus, Nestor's Grandson," XXXII). This story offers Fénelon's portrait of a jaded young man, who, after having been granted by Athena the freedom to taste "the sweetness of sensual pleasures," finally learns the meaning of life through duty and service (6, 222). Neleus becomes the incarnation of the battle between the spirit and the flesh, the example of one who triumphs over pleasure and sybaritic indulgence. More fortunate than Alfaroute or Callimaque, he manages to escape the web of boredom and disillusion. Neleus is in this respect something of an earlier sketch for Idomeneus, one of the kings in *Télémaque*, the embodiment of the enlightened ruler, one who becomes aware of the dangers of luxury and materialism.

F. *"Les Aventures d'Aristonoüs"*

"Les Aventures d'Aristonoüs" ("The Adventures of Aristonoüs," XXXVI), the longest of the *Fables*, was originally published in 1699 under the title *Sophronyme*. It appeared subsequently in numerous eighteenth and nineteenth-century editions as a companion piece to both the *Dialogue des morts* and *Télémaque*. In this story Fénelon's hero serves as an illustration of how a person, although a victim of life's changing fortunes, can exemplify the qualities of kindness, generosity, and gratitude. Abandoned by his parents, sold into slavery, and later scorned by his brothers who become nonetheless the recipients of his aid, Aristonoüs displays until the end his innate goodness and his strengths of character. His virtue, however, does not go without its reward: Aristonoüs ultimately finds friendship, loyalty, and a reflection of his own virtue in Sophronyme, the grandson of his former benefactor, whom he chances to meet on the island of Delos.

Léon Boulvé, in his study of Fénelon's Hellenism, considers this narrative to be his most successful fictional attempt at joining ancient form with Christian thought. He sees the pagan as being represented not only by the Hellenic and Virgilian images of nature, but also by the serene stoicism of Aristonoüs. As for the Christian elements, Boulvé points to Sophronyme as a pious, solitary spirit who relates the magnificence of nature to its creator and to Aristonoüs as a symbol of forgiveness.[9] It might be well to add that "Les Aventures d'Aristonoüs" is quite possibly Fénelon's most romantic bit of storytelling. Encased with a veneer of the sentimental and enlivened by such Byzantine devices as shipwreck (Sophronyme's son is the victim) and separated families, this fable discloses Fénelon's debt to older fictional forms and his propensity for what a later generation will refer to as sensibility.

G. *Evaluation of the* Fables

Fénelon never really achieved any lasting fame either as a *conteur* (storyteller) or as a fabulist. To his credit it must be remembered, however, that in no way did he envision these stories as any great artistic success and therefore more than likely considered them as a collection which did not merit close critical scrutiny. In fact, it is generally agreed that Fénelon never intended the *Fables* to be published; they were not written at one definite time, but designed as compositions to fit the needs of day-to-day instruction. It is this absence of unity, at least in part, that accounts for the marked repetitive quality of the *Fables*, although some critics readily point out their variety of form and subject matter.[10]

If this collection possesses little intrinsic value, it must still be viewed as a noteworthy step in the evolution of Fénelon's thought and imaginative powers. It is something of a point of departure for his subsequent excursions in the field of pedagogical literature, for in the *Dialogues des morts* and in *Télémaque* he will reintroduce in a different form and manner many of the same themes and ideas: the evils of luxurious living, the advantages of a simple, natural existence, the horror of war, and the benevolence of kings. The *Fables* must also be considered within a certain historical context. Fénelon should be counted among those few seventeenth-century writers who contributed to children's literature. Although not intended for a mass readership (in fact, written for a privileged individual, and because of this factor still considered by some to be an isolated exception),[11] Fénelon's work in this particular genre deserves its rightful place and the benefits of an unbiased reading.

II *The* Dialogues des morts *(Dialogues of the Dead)*

In order to provide additional material, both engaging and instructive, for a student who was fast becoming an adolescent,
Fénelon turned his attention, possibly around 1692 or 1693, to a
time-honored composition, the dialogue of the dead. Lucian, the
second-century Greek satirist, had long been recognized as the
creator of this very particular literary form, one which had been
masterfully exploited by such French writers as Boileau (*Dialogue
des héros de roman*, written c. 1665) and Fontenelle (*Dialogues des
morts*, 1683). Fénelon, though obviously not an admirer of Lucian's
anti-Christian spirit, recognized the possibilities of the genre: two or
more interlocutors, stripped of their rank and power by death the
great equalizer, meet and converse in the Elysian Fields; they may
be ancient or modern personages, and they may represent lands
both far away and near. This special sort of cadre is appealing to the
reader, since it gives him the feeling that he is listening to a real
conversation instead of being involved in formal study.[12]

Of the seventy-nine extant dialogues, fifty-one are dialogues of
the ancients, twenty-seven are dialogues of the moderns, and one
(LII) is a dialogue of an ancient and a modern. John Cosentini, in his
study of the *Dialogues*, reminds us that actually not all of Fénelon's
interlocutors are dead, for he counts eleven dialogues that feature participants who are portrayed as still alive.[13] The
Dialogue des morts began to appear in 1700, when four (XXI,
XXXVII, LXIV, and LXXIV) were printed; then, in 1712, forty-five
were published in an edition that was more than likely edited by the
Jesuit Father Tournemine. New additions were included in Ramsay's 1718 edition, bringing the total to sixty-six. A few more were
published in volume IV of the Querbeuf edition in 1787 and the
remainder in volume XIX of the Versailles edition of 1823.

A. *Warning for a Young Prince*

One of the aims of Fénelon's indirect instruction in the *Dialogues*
is to show the Duc de Bourgogne the image of what he might
become should he forget the wise counsel given to him during his
youth. In the first dialogue of the collection, which among other
things helps to set the mood and tone for the rest of the imaginary
conversations, Charon, the ferryman of the river Styx, learns from
Mercury that Prince Picrochole (a name which Fénelon must surely

have borrowed from either Rabelais or La Fontaine as a pseudonym for his pupil) will not be joining them in the underworld. Even though he is prone to exaggerate his minor illnesses, and subject to anger, laziness, and rebelliousness, the young prince, in Mercury's eyes, shows great promise. The important factor is that, like the youthful Achilles, he too has a Chiron and a Phoenix (an obvious reference to the Duc de Beauvillier and Fénelon, it would seem); and that under their guidance he should overcome his quick temper and his idleness and continue to improve in temperament and character. As Consentini concludes, this composition is scarcely a true dialogue, since there is neither a dispute nor a conflict of ideas; it is "rather an exhortation addressed to the Duke by Fénelon."[14]

The dialogue concerning Picrochole is, however, only a prelude to other colloquies in which Fénelon, while stressing the importance of one's formative years, points to well-known examples of men who did not heed the lessons of their youth. Achilles is a case in point. Lamenting his impetuous, immoderate behavior while he was among the living, he appears before his mentor Chiron (III) only to be told that a high-spirited young person must believe wise people, profit from past mistakes in order to avoid those of the future, and "invoke often the aid of Minerva whose wisdom is superior to the unbridled importance of Mars" (6, 236). In much the same vein is a dialogue in which Alcibiades is rebuked by Socrates (XVI) for having dishonored his philosophical education; and still another in which Alexander is reminded by his former teacher Aristotle (XXV) that, despite his exemplary youth, the famous world conqueror became a man given to ostentation, cruelty, and anger. When asked by Alexander why it is that one is so well behaved during one's early years and so injudicious as an adult, the philosopher, in words that summarize Fénelon's attitude, replies: "It is during youth that a person is taught, encouraged, and corrected by people of merit. Later on, one becomes prey to three sorts of enemies: presumption, passion, and flattery" (6, 269).

B. *The Demands of Kingship*

The greatest share by far of Fénelon's effort in the *Dialogues des morts* is reserved for his elucidation of those qualities that a good ruler should possess as well as those he should disdain. The demands of kingship call for, first of all, an adherence to a specific mode of personal conduct. What Fénelon advocates in a general sense is the adoption of a moral code, the touchstone of which is an all-embracing concept of virtue. Although he does not formally define this attribute (perhaps better expressed in English as moral strength or courage) for his young prince, he clearly indicates (XXI), for example, that virtue "is insensitive to riches and pleasure"; and that at the same time it is "sensitive to honor, justice, and friendship" (6, 265). Socrates, in his encounter with Alcibiades referred to above (XVI), shames the profligate Athenian for having been motivated by ambition instead of a love of virtue. Such a man, says the philosopher, cannot hope for any sort of honorable reputation. Everything considered, virtue, as Scipio Africanus points out to Hannibal (XXXVIII), becomes its own reward, causing one eventually to spurn any other sort of recompense.

There are, however, less abstract, but equally desirable qualities that Fénelon brings to the attention of his pupil. Most of these admirable traits are to be found in the person of Henri IV, who comes the closest to the author's idea of the perfect monarch. In a dialogue of striking contrast (LXVIII), he gives his cousin, the effeminate and dissolute Henri III, a miniature lesson, interspersed with historical allusion, on the conduct of kings. A head of state must be sincere, just, and frank; he must place himself, through upright behavior and honorable mores, in a position where he can trust men; above all, he must always think of the welfare of his people. This concept of benevolence is also underscored in an earlier dialogue (XXIII). Here Plato tells Dionysius II, the Syracusan tyrant of the fourth century B. C., that if a king has the love of his subjects, then he has no need of guards; he stands "like a father who fears nothing in the midst of his own children" (6, 267). The contract between ruler and ruled thus becomes one of mutual sympathy and understanding; it is, in other words, an exchange of loyal, devoted service for admiration and respect.

Such rulers as the good and wise Henri IV, however, are greatly outnumbered by an array of tyrants, dictators, generals, emperors, ministers, and kings who were motivated by unsound and dangerous principles. In summoning forth the likes of Romulus, Alexander, Nero, Caligula, and Julius Caesar, among others, Fénelon affords his student a rather substantial catalogue of faults which should be spurned and pitfalls which should be avoided. Fénelon speaks at length, for example, of the pernicious effects of flattery (XXI,

LXXVII); condemns the bellicose, imperialistic spirit of all kings (X); denounces the betrayal of one's country (LXXVI and XXXIV); cautions against gluttony (XXX, XL), the love of pleasure (XX), and the "shameful passion for women" (LXII).

When the preceptor turns his attention to Louis XI (1423–1483), he seems to find the very epitome of the dark, evil, and imperfect king; appearing in more dialogues (LVII, LVIII, LIX, LX, LXI, LXXV) than any other personage, Louis XI stands quite possibly as the blackest villain to parade across the pages of the *Dialogues des morts*. It is Louis XI's reign, as we hear of it, that furnishes proof enough that a king cannot and should not be tyrannical, cruel, proud, and deceitful. The long list of grievances drawn up against him by Cardinal Balue (LVIII) is in essence a crushing diatribe unmitigated by any sort of constructive criticism. Fénelon seems to ignore the possibility that unscrupulous and treacherous rulers could also be capable administrators; he has quickly forgotten that Louis XI should be praised for his unification of France, his economic policies, and his introduction of printing into the country. In short, Fénelon gives no quarter to any tyrant.

In other dialogues (XII, XLII) he underscores, as Plato does in *The Republic*, the self-destructive, almost criminal force that sweeps such a man to eventual ruin. Although Fénelon believes that a monarch is a safeguard against anarchy, he goes so far as to suggest that a tyrant might very well perform one last, decent act by abdicating (XLI, XLIV). Absolutism, to Fénelon, is not synonymous with tyranny; it is, however, a form of government that must be administered through wisdom, patience, and justice.

C. *Literature, Eloquence, and Art*

Although Fénelon does not grant a preeminent place in the *Dialogues des morts* to artistic and literary matters, he does demonstrate, through numerous citations and references, his love and knowledge of ancient letters. In two dialogues, moreover, he goes beyond a simple or fleeting allusion to reveal at least a small part of his literary judgment. When Achilles chances to meet Homer (IV), Fénelon weaves into their discussion his own comparison of *The Iliad* and *The Odyssey*. Achilles' declaration that the story of Ulysses is "nothing more than an accumulation of old wives' tales" ("un amas de contes de vieilles," 6, 236) elicits from the blind poet a reminder that an author must vary his style according to his subject matter. Calypso and Nausicaa, he maintains, cannot be depicted in the same heroic fashion as the gods and heroes who fought at Troy's gates.

This same question of genre and style is of primary importance in the one remaining literary dialogue (LI). Here Fénelon imagines a meeting between Horace and Virgil, but this time there is no need for a clash of personalities or the rattle of polemical swords. Each poet praises the other for the variety of his works; each considers that the other possesses great versatility. The dialogue does not end without a certain tension, however, for the two writers are finally willing to speak of defects: Horace finds, for example, that Virgil is more elegant, more polished, more refined than Homer, but at the same time less simple, less vigorous and sublime. Virgil, for his part, suggests that some of Horace's phrases are too neatly turned; and that despite the brevity and delicacy which his words convey, there is a lack of uniformity to the smoothness of their flow. This encounter between the two Roman poets is handled with great charm and feeling; its ease and elegance is in many ways a welcome relief from the disputatious, tendentious atmosphere of so many of the other dialogues. The literary criticism presented here is of a type that is new to the dialogue form: "Boileau criticized by satirizing; Fénelon openly presents the writers discussing their works."[15]

The spirit of amicability that reigns in the dialogue between Horace and Virgil is missing in the three dialogues (XXXI, XXXII, XXXIII) that are devoted to the subject of oratory and eloquence. Demosthenes and Cicero, the interlocutors for this particular series, exchange rather acicular reflections and observations about each other's accomplishments and characteristics. In tracing this parallel, Fénelon leaves little doubt that he is giving the edge in this debate to Demosthenes. Cicero is portrayed as a rather vain and conceited ("I have composed works which will last for all time," 6, 274) man who boasts of the fertility of his genius, of the spirit, facility, and feeling present in his orations. Demosthenes, on the other hand, defends the Fénelonian canon of simplicity ("True eloquence seeks to hide its art," 6, 274), and the aesthetic principle that disinterestedness creates perfection. Here in the *Dialogues des morts* Fénelon no longer manifests that great measure of admiration for Cicero that is so evident in the *Dialogues sur l'éloquence;* instead, he reinforces his strong attachment to a Platonic concept, expressed by Demosthenes in the following manner: "The true use of eloquence [is] to publish truth and to convince others that justice and the other virtues are the truly useful qualities . . ." (6, 276).

Fénelon's attention to the visual arts is represented by two dialogues in which Nicolas Poussin (1594–1665), one of his preferred painters, converses first with Parrhasius (LII), the Greek artist who flourished c. 400 B. C., and then with the better-known Leonardo da Vinci (LII).[16] The first of these dialogues gives every promise of being a thoroughly interesting debate on the subject of the relative excellence of ancient and modern painting; very soon, however, Parrhasius asks Poussin to describe for him his painting *The Funeral of Phocion*. At this point the dialogue has virtually only one speaker, Poussin, and what we have "is a very interesting essay on the masterpiece of the French painter."[17] This purely expository quality is carried over into the companion dialogue with Leonardo. Poussin analyzes for the Italian one of his landscapes, comparing it just as favorably with the painting of the other dialogue. While these discourses may be looked on as Fénelon's bid to give his student "a lesson in art appreciation,"[18] it is also possible to interpret them as the author's revelation of his concept of ancient Greece, "a completely intellectual creation" of Athens and the antique world.[19] These dialogues also have an historical significance in that they disclose Fénelon's role as an early art critic; among French writers he must certainly be considered as one of the first to have placed, as the noted French literary historian Gustave Lanson says, "literature and the arts in communication."[20]

D. *Among the Philosophers*

Five of the dialogues in the collection dramatize the encounters of a select group of philosophical figures. Of the seven philosophers who appear in this series, only two—Socrates and Plato—emerge unscathed from their verbal clashes. Aristotle, for example, is attacked by Plato, among other things, for his obscureness, for his failure to discuss "eternal ideas," and for the jargon-like quality of his *Physics* (XXXIV); Pyrrho is ridiculed by an unnamed shade for his sceptical, nihilistic doctrine (XXIX); and Descartes is confronted by Aristotle who is quite unreceptive to his theory of animal automatism (LXXVIII). Cicero, making another appearance in the *Dialogues*, receives a sound tongue-lashing from Cato, who derides his philosophical wavering, his lack of originality ("Admit it openly, you were nothing more than a feeble copier of the Greeks," 6, 291), and his political duplicity (XLIII).

Of this group the dialogue between Socrates and Confucius (VII) is not only the longest, but the most interesting. Cynical and pessimistic about the ultimate effect that philosophical teaching has had on society in general ("I am so disillusioned about the human race that a general reform of a republic appears to me impossible," 6, 241), Socrates quickly concludes that Confucius' notion cannot be judged superior to that of any other race or nation. His expository speeches reveal in some detail his scorn for Chinese culture and civilization; the Greek philosopher remains completely unimpressed with China's contributions to the areas of mathematics, astronomy, printing, porcelain-making, architecture, and painting. Although Fénelon had for a good while been haunted by a marvellous, idealized image of the Orient, his posture here seems to represent a reaction against the veneration of certain Jesuit missionaries (with whom he had had some direct contacts) for Chinese mores and thought.[21] Sceptical, at least for the moment, Fénelon holds in check that esteem for the wise and learned Confucius which was to become an accepted eighteenth-century attitude.

E. *Ulysses et Grillus*

The dialogue between Ulysses and Grillus (VI) is not only one of the best of the collection from the standpoint of form, but it is also one of the most provocative in thought.[22] Although the basic frame of the story appears in both Homer and Plutarch, Fénelon may possibly have borrowed the idea from La Fontaine's "Les Compagnons d'Ulysse" (*Fables*, XII, 1), which had been published as early as 1690 in the *Mercure Galant*.[23]

The hero of *The Odyssey*, at the moment we see him, has succeeded in freeing his fellow travelers from Circe's spell. Grillus, however, refuses to assume his former shape, preferring to remain a pig; so it is that Ulysses must convince him that human form and activity are suitable and advantageous. He does not have an easy time of it, for Grillus engages in a clever rebuttal to all his arguments: man's nobility, he says, is an illusion, and all his misfortunes are real; as an animal, his needs are simple, and he is, moreover, free; his present tastes do not cater to literature and the arts, and he cannot trust the science of medicine. What does it matter if he is transformed into hams and sausages? Man, too, will meet his end; and he will do so after a life devoid of happiness and sensual ease. Humans do not possess that wisdom which makes them the equal of the gods; they are, on the contrary, unjust, deceitful, cruel, and blind. At least a pig is innocent and holds no malice; he is honest, unambitious, and seeks no unjust conquest; he is content to eat, drink, and sleep, leaving the rest of the world in peace.

Despite these excellent rejoinders by Grillus, Ulysses tries one final argument: is it possible that one can renounce that one gift— immortality—which places man in a position far above that of the lower animals? Grillus' reply to this consideration is a rather long speech which ends the dialogue. He wishes to be shown if man possesses a true immortality. He insists on seeing in this life after death something real, something more noble than the present bodily form ("this uncouth and disturbed machine," 6, 240). Will he be truly happy if he achieves this immortality, or will he be no more than the victim of unjust gods?

In this debate which Fénelon maintains until the end of the dialogue, there is no moralistic conclusion.[24] We can deduce, however, from the abundant implications here that man can aspire to something better than a pagan, epicurean existence. His works, his dreams, his hopes have no meaning unless they are based on a scheme "which receives its sanction from a supernatural source; unless the end of that scheme is supernatural existence, and man's contingent nature and acts find their justification in an eternal and divine plan."[25] There will always be Grillus-like people in the world, Fénelon seems to be saying, and it is perhaps this idea that gives the dialogue its very somber and pessimistic quality.

F. *Evaluation of the* Dialogues des morts

The critical reaction to the *Dialogues des morts* has never been marked by unanimity of opinion. Among Fénelon's contemporaries the work does not seem to have been too warmly received. Bossuet, for example, on reading the first four dialogues, which were published in 1700, was reported to have said that they were nothing more than "insults which the interlocutors exchanged with each other."[26] What we know of eighteenth-century criticism is scarcely any better: both Cardinal Maury and La Harpe, whose reactions have survived, accused Fénelon of having sacrificed historical truth to pedagogical goals.[27] Then, of course, the deliberate tampering with Fénelon's text by a succession of editors prior to 1823 in no way contributed to the luster of an already dubious reputation. Gradually, at any rate, the *Dialogues* came to be accepted as something of a classic example of pedagogical literature; they came to be viewed, for all intents and purposes, as an interesting illustration of Fénelon's theory of an "attractive" education, but a work, however, which could lay but little claim to any sort of elevated position in French letters.

Only during the last twenty-five years or so have critics really been disposed to view the *Dialogues* from a perspective other than the strictly pedagogical. The praise for Fénelon's variety of tone, his verve, his skillful use of historical anecdote, and what he calls his "novelistic" gifts is certainly a perceptive judgment, one which should not be taken, I feel, as shallow encomium.[28] This opinion contrasts, however, very sharply with an earlier notion of the uneven, fragmentary quality of the *Dialogues*.[29] Cosentini's 1959 article is also a valuable study in that it diverts our attention, for the intents, by concentrating most part at least, from Fénelon's didactic on a study of the form of the dialogues. Although Cosentini speaks of Fénelon's "anxiety to drive home the point clearly and unequivocally," he demonstrates how he is able in at least ten of the dialogues (VI, XI, XXXVII, LVII, for example) to do justice to the form.[30] In those particular compositions, as he says, Fénelon affords the reader the necessary qualities of the genre—"characterization, clash of ideas, dramatic and lively debate, comical touches."[31] Even so, Cosentini is basically unwilling to judge Fénelon except by those standards that apply to his contemporary Fontenelle, whom he considers the most skilled writer in the genre. As Robert Paul Holley observes (in his 1971 doctoral dissertation), the dialogues of Fontenelle may be "better literature," but "those of Fénelon show a greater unity between matter and form."[32] Holley also calls to our attention such matters as Fénelon's use of historical figures, pointing out that his aim "is to judge them and not to arrive like Fontenelle at a brilliant epigram."[33]

Fénelon is, no doubt, indebted to both Fontenelle and Lucian, but his position in the genre is something resembling an intermediary one. When he prefers, Fénelon is quite capable of making use of Lucian's technique of direct attack; on the other hand, it appears that he has imitated Fontenelle in the use of two historical personages and the inclusion of notable people who have not long been dead.[34] The question of whether or not Fénelon has transformed the Lucianic *isotomia* into a markedly Christian concept is, of course, debatable. I am more inclined to accept Holley's view that here in the *Dialogues* there is an idea of reward and punishment after death, but that "the Christian concept of union with God in eternal happiness is completely absent."[35]

On at least one point, however, most critics seem to agree: the *Dialogues des morts*, like the *Fables*, is a work which constitutes an introduction to *Télémaque*, "a kind of foretaste of its principal lesson."[36] Fénelon's ideas, particularly certain political ones, have passed the stage of germination. They have grown to the point where he is now ready to transplant them to still another fictional cadre. From the history and drama of his underworld characters we shall pass to a Homeric world where the lure and charm of new adventures provide still further lessons for a very special student.

CHAPTER 4

The Mystic Call

I The Background to Quietism

QUIETISM, that form of mysticism which claims that the soul, in
a state of absolute "quiet" or rest, is capable of being absorbed
by a type of passive and permanent contemplation that allows it to
attain God's grace, was in no way an isolated segment of theological
thought or feeling. It did not, in other words, one day appear as a
doctrine suddenly invented and professed by Madame Guyon. To
trace its origins in rapid order is no easy task, for it is a link in what
has been described as "the great mystic chain" which stretches
throughout the ages.[1] Fénelon, like all the great mystics, was aware
of the basic conformity of his thought with most of his predecessors.
To the end he remained convinced that his interpretation of "pure
love" was the outcome of a long tradition. Behind him lay a whole
body of theology reaching as far back in time as Clement of Alexandria (c. 160–220) and extending into the present to encompass François de Sales (1567–1622).

France had experienced, certainly as early as the waning years of
the sixteenth century, a religious revival which bore in its own way a
mystical imprint. In particular, the veneration of the faithful for
devout souls and the love for devotional writers would be bequeathed to the new century. Beginning in 1601 with Jean Quin-
tinadoine de Bretigny and Dom du Chèvre's translation of the works
of Saint Teresa and continuing for at least two decades, the French-
man would be able to read in his native tongue a wide variety of
works by those we consider the great mystics: Richard Beaucousin's
1606 version of Ruysbroeck; Jean-Baptiste de Machault's translation
of Harphius, the first complete one to appear in French (1617); and
René Gaulthier's 1621 edition of John of the Cross (1542–1591), to
name but a few.[2]

74

At the same time the devout were poring over these new discoveries, they were able to avail themselves of the works of a group of new writers who were creating little by little a body of original spiritual works. The first of note is Laurent de Paris' *Le Palais d'amour divin (The Palace of Divine Love)* (1602), in which the mystical element was more than abundantly represented by his concern for humility, contrition, and that specific quality to be talked about so much in the following years: *anéantissement* or the annihilation, the reduction, the stripping away of one's confidence and self-esteem to the point that only God's help and support are sought. A bit later, in 1608, Pierre Coton's *Intérieure Occupation d'une âme dévote (Interior Occupation of a Devout Soul)* stressed the important doctrine of *abandon*—that almost natural accompaniment of *anéantissement*—which held that complete trust in and surrender to God's will would lead to the happiness and joy visible in one's childhood.

A year after the *Intérieure Occupation*, the English Capuchin Benoit Canfield's *Règle de perfection (Rule of Perfection)* appeared in a French edition.[3] The mystic voluntaryism of this abstract work, one of the most successful of its kind published in the seventeenth century, was to exert great influence on Madame Guyon who incorporated a whole chapter of it in her *Justifications*. The basic idea of Canfield's spiritual progression is framed within the perspective of a union of man's will to what he calls the three wills of God: exterior will, or one's active life; interior will, or the contemplative side of man's life; and essential will, or sureminent life.

The growth of mysticism in this early period was also profoundly shaped by the work of a highly significant figure, François de Sales. After reconciling the Christian life with that of the world in his *Introduction à la vie dévote (Introduction to the Devout Life, 1609)*, he turned, perhaps under the influence of Jean-Pierre Camus (1582–1653), the Bishop of Belley, to mystic thought, producing the *Traité de l'amour de Dieu (Treatise on the Love of God)* in 1616. The originality of his theological position is to be explained by the fact that he accorded an important place to contemplation, that "loving, simple, and permanent attention of the mind to divine matters," and placed mysticism on a personal level, divorced from the obscurantism of Canfield's abstract school.[4] Saint François, centering his doctrine on the love of God, marked out in steps how those

who were desirous of perfection might pass from a "holy resignation" to a "very holy indifference." For him mystic theology had as
its goal the direction of souls, through the practice of prayer
(*oraison*) and the Christian virtues, toward the perfection of love,
the crowning achievement of which was the possession of God in
heaven.[5]

All this outpouring of mystical thought did not remain for long
without opposition. Whether because of the exaggeration of vocabulary ("indifférence" and "abandon," for example) or because of
general misunderstanding on the part of the uninitiated, there arose
from certain orthodox quarters a concern about all this new spiritual
activity. In 1623 Cardinal Pacheco, the Inquisitor-General, published in Seville an edict condemning, among others, the "Alumbrados" or "Illuminated Ones." Almost a decade later this same
group, some of whom had been driven out of Spain, were attacked
by a Capuchin priest, Archange Ripault. The antimystical campaign
was also carried into the Jansenist camp where suspicions of strange
spiritual power fell upon its director, the Abbé de Saint-Cyran, who
was jailed on orders from Cardinal Richelieu in 1638. While this
great religious leader languished in his Vincennes prison, the Jesuit
Antoine Sirmond attacked François de Sales' disciple Camus, referred to above, who had just published his *Défense du pur amour*
(1640). Fénelon, who later chose to refer to Camus (see 2, 635; 636)
in the midst of his own struggle, was well aware that the latter's
polemical battles were a prefiguration of his own with Bossuet.

It was not only in France and Spain that mystic and antimystic
carried out their heated debates. Italy, too, proved to be a favorable
climate for the development of Quietist or semi-Quietist views. One
of the most notable representatives of that country's interest in the
spirituality of "abandonment" was Giovanni Falconi, (d. 1632) who
has been called "the father of modern Quietism." Recommending
for the devout a state of peace, rest, and silence, he also spoke of
abandon, not as a transitory mystical act, but as one which should be
continuous—a type of permanent union, that is, with God. Falconi
attempted to avoid the charge of personal irresponsibility or immo-
rality by admitting that the soul, even though suspended in this
uninterrupted and inactive fashion, was capable of falling from this
mystical state into sin through the commission of some grave error.
Falconi becomes most prominent in the history of Quietism when
we realize that it was his theories that were taken up and developed

not only in France by François Malaval (1627–1719), but by the Spaniard Miguel de Molinos.[6]

The term Quietism seems, in fact, to have been first used, sometime around 1680, in the midst of the conflict over Molinism.[7] Had it not been for the furor caused by the teachings of that Spanish priest who was born in Saragossa in 1640, Madame Guyon might possibly have come to be accepted as nothing short of a saint, and Fénelon could have, no doubt, continued to enjoy the esteem and confidence of the mighty. Molinos himself was for some while highly regarded; the publication of his *Guida spirituale (Spiritual Guide)* in Rome in 1675 was well received by both clergy and laymen. Cardinal d'Estrées, at that time the French ambassador to Italy, was convinced that the acceptance of Molinos' ideas was a sure means of leading the Protestants back to the fold.[8] Fashionable and accepted, Molinos' new doctrine eventually evoked the concern of the Jesuits and Dominicans, who had become alarmed at the wholesale defection of their spiritual advisees to the camp of this new religion. Although their efforts to suppress the *Guida* and to stifle its influence failed, continued reports about the dark and secret side of Molinism, which recalled for some the activities of the "Alumbrados" as well as the mystic rapture of the fourteenth-century Beghards, succeeded in keeping the controversy alive. In France Father La Chaise informed the king of the new danger. Louis XIV then urged d'Estrées to see the Pope. Innocent XI in turn referred the ambassador, now perfectly willing to forsake his former friend, to the Inquisition. As a result of an examination of that body, Molinos was arrested in July, 1685, and his doctrine subsequently condemned.

It is not too difficult to understand why Molinos' theology was alarming from an orthodox point of view. It tended, in the first place, by advocating for the soul a state of absolute inaction (called "quietude" or "the interior way") to instill in man a great indifference for his salvation and for the essential practices of his religious life. Exterior works, including confession, were for Molinos only extraneous elements which were capable of distracting the devout from the perfect rest of contemplation. The soul, merged entirely in God, was to think no more of reward or punishment; it was to consider neither heaven nor hell, neither death nor eternity. In short, the resignation of the will to the Almighty made the Christian unaccountable even for the most sinful of acts; it was henceforth unnecessary to think of rewards, punishments—or even temptation. The body could well become the devil's domain, but the soul, united to its Creator, played no part in carnal matters.

II *Madame Guyon*

Jeanne-Marie Bouvier de la Motte-Guyon (1648–1717) would more than likely today be called in popular terms a cult figure. As such, it is no small wonder that she has, through the years, been maligned and for the most part misunderstood. A neurotic she may have been; but, everything considered, she does not deserve the black reputation which Bossuet, ill-prepared—before the Issy Conferences at any rate—to speak at great length on mystical subjects, imposed upon her. Fénelon, as has been pointed out, would never have confided in her had he thought her either mad or immoral.[9] The fact is that, except for notable exceptions, she remains a writer whose works have been but little read and poorly studied. It must be said at the outset, moreover, that she never intended to propagate Molinism in France; hers was a more subtle, a more spiritual doctrine of the soul's perfection.

Drawn to mysticism by a cold, unhappy marriage as well as no doubt by her very nature, Madame Guyon was indoctrinated by spiritual directors whose beliefs were influenced by the abstract school of the early seventeenth century. Centered about the teachings of Madame Acarie (1566–1618) and Canfield, this group sought through the spirituality of annihilation a sublime or ethereal life devoid of all conceptual elements. So it is at the outset that we find Madame Guyon's doctrine far less original than some might believe. On the other hand, she was influenced, more than the other mystics of her time, by the Spanish school, particularly by Saint John of the Cross. Madame Guyon was one of the first to see in mysticism an experimental seizure of God's presence and to speak of "an experimental taste" of the Almighty's presence.[10] In this respect she pushes beyond the psychomystical tendencies of Saint Teresa. There is in this approach a basic simplicity that may seem to clash with her abstractiveness and her psychologism: at the base of her system is the belief that the soul, reconstructed in an interior fashion by God and transformed into Him, sees only God in everything. Her notion of divine immanence is founded on the ambiguous principle that God is in us more than we are ourselves. Once the soul strips away the will and the ego, it is God and God is the soul.[11] So far as prayer is concerned, Madame Guyon holds that it is a state, not an act; it is God within us who prays through His spirit. The unique rule governing this activity is the submission (or a type of linking) of human will to divine will.[12]

This simplicity is, in fact, Madame Guyon's token of moral perfection. The soul in its mystic quest must, through divine justice and wisdom, cast aside all "property," or in other words "disappropriate" itself of any earthly or carnal elements. Indifference, for her, is the mark of supreme annihilation.[13] Thus, as the soul is elevated, God's action within it becomes more apparent. Gradually, the soul, sensing that it is God who is acting, enters the domain of passivity.

As Cognet concludes, Madame Guyon's mysticism is essentially one of annihilation through depersonalization. It is hard to believe that she ever considered the union of God and man as being a real hypostatic coalition. She is in fact a theorist of the theopathic state, one which is composed of stable and permanent realities, and which places the soul in a position where sin is practically impossible. Perhaps her greatest doctrinal error is her insistence on placing man in contact with the divine in a direct manner rather than through an intermediary. The minimal place that she accords the humanity of Christ is also a contentious area, despite her cult for childhood and her devotion to the infant Jesus.[14]

III *Fénelon's Mysticism Before the* Maximes

Although Fénelon himself disavowed any sort of contact with mysticism before 1684, it is generally assumed that at least as early as his seminary days he had been introduced by his spiritual guide Tronson to the mystic fervor of the writings of Olier, the founder of Saint-Sulpice. Later, while drafting his *Réfutation de Malebranche*, Fénelon seemed to discover another element, "another mystical tendency" of his own philosophy: completely permeated by the concept of divine infinity, he made known his opposition to any sort of order that limited God.[15] Be that as it may, Madame Guyon must surely be given a fair amount of credit for rekindling whatever latent mysticism he possessed. She was in a limited but important manner the catalyst that set in motion his exploration of the interior life. It was as if he recognized that her doctrine—at least in part—had already been his for some while.[16]

In this early period, then, before the Issy Conferences, the influence of Madame Guyon was perhaps more emotional than it was theological. As much as anything it was her presence, her saintly image, her lack of austerity, and her nonintellectual approach to religion that led Fénelon to take the first step in his spiritual evolution. Everything considered, "He had faith in her before he put his confidence in her doctrine."[17] Their correspondence covering the years 1688–89[18] reveals the admiration and ease with which Fénelon allowed himself to be conquered. He may have had reservations about some of her concepts; he may have asked for explanations, but in the end he allowed his faith in her to silence his doubts.

Up to now there had been no quarrel over Quietism. That was to begin the day that, Madame Guyon, expelled from Saint-Cyr, would ask that her ideas be examined and evaluated. The period of the Issy Conferences marked, therefore, a new state in Fénelon's development. It is characterized, first of all, by his cautionary, discreet approach to the doctrinal problems of the issue and, secondly, by the quick assumption on his part of a defensive spirit. These attitudes are manifest in at least two rather significant works which he produced mainly for the benefit of Bossuet, Noailles, and Tronson. Convinced that he should rest his case—and Madame Guyon's for that matter—on tradition, that is, on the support of orthodox, but mystic figures of both the remote and not-so-distant past, Fénelon began by drafting for the commissioners a *Mémoire sur l'état passif (Memoir on the Passive State)*. In this work, which he never saw fit to publish, he attempted to show that perfect indifference and passive prayer are states of the soul which control each other in a reciprocal manner. They are for all practical purposes terms that "are truly synonymous."[19] Assuming that the Christian has thrown aside his own will, and therefore that God's will now dominates his heart, then one can suppose that he is in a state of total renunciation of self and others as well as in a state of contemplation (or contemplative prayer). To justify this position, Fénelon first calls upon François de Sales and John of the Cross, whose teachings, he reminds his critics, are above any sort of suspicion. If the modern Church approves the doctrine of such men, one can conclude, states Fénelon quite categorically, that it is "either an express revelation of the Scripture or else a foundation in the depth of its mysteries."[20] Fénelon also cites other authorities, including Saint Paul (1 Corinthians: II, 15), Saint John (I John: II, 20), and Saint Augustine *(Confessions: IX, 10)*.

The above *Mémoire* also includes a passage which glorifies Saint Clement of Alexandria, whose philosophy became the subject of still another work. Written probably during July and August of 1694, *Le Gnostique de Saint Clément d'Alexandrie (The Gnosticism of Saint Clement of Alexandria)* is Fénelon's best-developed and most synthetic response of this period.[21] In turning to Saint Clement, Fénelon seizes upon the doctrine of one whom he believed faithful to Catholic tradition. The Gnosticism or knowledge of spiritual truth of this early Christian figure was to Fénelon's mind a true one, for it was based not on pride or pleasurable sensations, but on the perfect life of the spirit. From the *Stromateis* of Clement's successor Origen, Fénelon drew out the references to contemplation, both the Platonic (aspiration toward the supreme Good) and the Pythagorean (the *epopteia* or contemplation of nature) varieties. His basic conclusions are perhaps best stated in the following passage:

He [the Gnostic] has no further need of virtue, for having no longer any sort of evil to combat, he remains apathetic and imperturbable; his contemplation has become a live and permanent substance . . . He is the very soul of goodness. He has no further desire to formulate either earthly goods or his own salvation . . . so much is his love disinterested . . . Finally, he desires nothing, not even for his perseverance; for when one has entered into the divine part of love, perfect love is no longer a desire, but a union of a unity which is fixed and tranquil.[22]

To Fénelon's mind this state constituted a type of stability which was symbolic of ideal spirituality.

Fénelon's systematizing of Clement's theology was scarcely acceptable to Bossuet. Although the latter in no way denied that this apostolic figure was orthodox, he refused to approve Fénelon's interpretation of Gnosticism. In his *Tradition des nouveaux mystiques (Tradition of the New Mystics)*, Bossuet countered Fénelon's statements by asserting his belief in the perfection of the Christian through ordinary channels.[23] Madame Guyon's friend, he contended, had quite simply misinterpreted the text to the advantage of the mystics and their belief in a passive state. Most of all, Bossuet was disturbed by Fénelon's insistence on a "secret tradition." Christian instruction in no way could be said to be incommunicable; the mysteries of the Church surely belonged to everyone. What is perhaps most interesting about this skirmish is the fact that Fénelon, to all indications, never read the Bishop of Meaux's *Tradition;*

he did, however, from this time on remain silent on the subject of the deep, secret, and hidden mysteries.[24] *Le Gnostique,* carefully and discreetly put aside, was not published until 1930.

There is another work that Fénelon did not choose to publish. It too is a product of the Issy Conferences, a firm indication of his latent dissatisfaction with the articles, despite the fact that he had approved them on March 10, 1695. At the same time it constitutes Fénelon's reaction to the incarceration of Madame Guyon at Vincennes in December of that year and mirrors to some degree his feeling that there might very well be a reprise of hostilities.[25] This document is the *Explication des Articles d'Issy (Explanation of the Issy Articles)* which he had prepared, in all likelihood, for Tronson and Noailles by March, 1696.

This *Explication,* a work almost totally eclipsed by the later *Explication des maximes des saints,* is more a commentary than a treatise; more a type of apology than a declaration. Generally speaking, the tone of Fénelon's discussion is "calm, conciliatory, insinuative."[26] He accepts the formula of each of the thirty-four articles, except for the ninth which states: "It is not permitted for a Christian to be indifferent either with regard to his salvation or to things which have a bearing on it: holy Christian indifference concerns the events of this life, except for sin, and the dispensation of spiritual comforts or discomforts."[27] On this point, Fénelon shows his reserve by maintaining that holy indifference "extends much farther than the events of this life," and that the soul "prepossessed by pure love acts with the same disinterestedness and the same indifference for its own happy or unhappy eternity as if it were assured of eternal punishment. . . ."[28] Despite his outward adherence to the rest of the Issy doctrine, Fénelon fills the pages of the *Explication* with exceptions and special examples—preceded by such qualifying words as "no doubt" and "but"—which he finds applicable to mysticism. Fénelon, clever and ingenious, is in effect hiding himself behind the thirty-four articles. Like the proverbial fox, he has infiltrated the hen house, but only, as it were, to survey the scene. Fénelon realized well enough that his reply was insufficient. At this point he could not risk falling into Bossuet's trap.

IV   *The* Explication des maximes des saints
(Explanation of the Maxims of the Saints)

As mentioned earlier, it took no more than the marginal citations of Bossuet's *Instruction sur les états d'oraison (Instruction on the*

States of Prayer), which fell under his glance that July of 1696, to convince Fénelon that he should prepare a true defense of his doctrine. He knew that he would have to furnish sooner or later a work to offset or at least to balance Bossuet's views. Acting swiftly, he wrote the book that was to become the most famous item of the Quietist quarrel—the *Explication des maximes des saints sur la vie intérieure.*

In the preface to the *Maximes* Fénelon reaffirms his belief that not all readers are prepared for a discussion of the interior life. The worldly and incredulous, he maintains, see in it only a source of derision, while the "credulous and indiscreet" accept it as a springboard to a life of visions and illusions. Despite his reticence to speak of such matters as disinterested love and contemplation, the time has come when he can no longer keep silent. He must now explain to mystics both "the experiences and the expressions of the saints" and clarify, moreover, "the true sense of these holy authors."[29] Fénelon also reveals that while examining the Issy articles in detail, he has formulated a basic thesis:

All interior ways tend toward pure or disinterested love; because they must always tend toward the highest perfection and because this pure love is the highest degree of Christian perfection. It is the terminus of all the ways which the saints have known . . . . This disinterested love, always inviolably attached to all of God's wills . . . performs the same acts and exercises all the same distinct virtues as interested love, with the sole difference that it usually carries them out in a simple, peaceful manner, separate from any motive of self-interest.[30]

Contemplation, too, even the most passive sort, in Fénelon's eyes is nothing except the peaceful and uniform exercise of this "pure love." "Only as one passes from interested love to the disinterested," he explains, "does one pass unknowingly from the meditation in which methodical and discursive acts are performed to contemplation whose acts are simple and direct."[31] In order to trace the pathway along which this spiritual progress is made, Fénelon has arranged his work as a series of forty-five articles designed to separate for the reader the false principles of mysticism from the true. Before proceeding to this task, he chooses to explain in a preliminary section the various meanings that can be assigned to the term "the love of God."

This exposition of a dozen pages or so divides the expression into five categories or states: (1) servile or carnal love, which is a type of self-love or the search for God's gifts; (2) the love of pure concupiscence, also a manifestation of self-interest and therefore an impious one; (3) the love of "hope," or a state wherein the soul truly loves God but without dominant or "effective" love; (4) a "mixed" love in which hope still occupies an important place; (5) the state of "pure love" or "perfect charity" in which the soul loves God only for Himself. The first three degrees are mentioned only insomuch as they show a gradation and thereby clearly mark the place of the last two. In fact, Fénelon's true aim in the *Maximes* is to show the distinction between the fourth and fifth degrees of love.[32]

In the main body of the *Maximes*, Fénelon seeks, then, to demonstrate that "pure love," the essential element of his mystical doctrine, is not a contradiction of the Christian life, but rather its highest and most supreme expression. "Pure love" is not, on the other hand, a perfection to which all souls can aspire. It is through God's grace that one can progressively achieve that desired mystic union, and no intervention except His is possible. Fénelon's doctrine hinges on the explanation of the following degrees of perfection which mark, like so many signposts, the Christian's journey toward total transformation:

(1) Disappropriation. For Fénelon the soul cannot expect to be reborn until it dies for itself. "Property," one of the major goals of the "love of hope," must disappear. Indifference or "holy indifference," as it is called, means that the mystic can have no more voluntary or deliberate desires for his interest. This does not imply a suspension of one's will with regard to salvation, for indifference is wanting what God wants. There is, moreover, no state of indifference "which gives souls a miraculous or extraordinary inspiration."[33]

(2) Trials *(Épreuves)*. The soul's special and difficult trials or tests are "nothing more than purification."[34] They are designed to help finish the process of disappropriation, to destroy all remnants of self-interest.

(3) Abandonment or surrender *(Abandon)*. Trials also contribute to placing the soul in a state of total surrender. By renouncing self-interest, it also is able to lose all hope of resourcefulness. Only on God can the soul be expected to lean. Even so, the soul must not count on any sort of divine support; it gives itself over to God's will, even with regard to its interest in eternal matters.

(4) Contemplation and passive contemplation. Fénelon endorses vocal prayer, just as he approves spiritual reading and meditation. Contemplation, however, is superior to these activities, for its acts, nondiscursive, "are so simple, so direct, so uniform that they have no marked quality by which they can be distinguished."[35] Capable of becoming passive, contemplation enters a pure state in which there is no natural activity. It is composed of acts of faith and love, "so peaceful and uniform" that they appear to the unknowing as one single act or as "a rest of pure union."[36]

(5) The passive state. Fénelon compares the simplicity of this particular state to that of childhood. Believing in no extraordinary inspiration, the soul allows itself to move, without reflection or resistance, with all the impressions of grace. Its passivity therefore possesses a real activity, although its will has been suppressed. Mystical union with God is now possible.

(6) Transformation. The soul, thus disposed, is now prepared for the ultimate spiritual union. God now lives within it and through it in a state, the most passive of all, which is capable of producing a foretaste of celestial beatitude. This transformation is neither a process of deification nor a hypostatic union; it is quite simply a state of "pure love" which alone composes the whole of the interior life, and "which then becomes the one and only principle of all intentional and meritorious acts."[37]

Such was Fénelon's subtle doctrine of the inner life, that zone of man's spiritual side which was able to coexist with his empirical personality. Although Fénelon repeats much of the classic formulas of mystical thought, he creates a system that is more fleeting and more intuitive than traditional doctrine.[38] At the same time he manages to refute more than a fair amount of Quietist beliefs. He condemns, for example, in Article II those who reject the idea of rewards; and in Article V he makes it clear that one "can never be in a state of real indifference or suspension with regard to salvation."[39] As cited earlier, he rejects (Article VII) the idea of miraculous or extraordinary inspiration. Fénelon also quite clearly separates his passivity *(passiveté)* from a state of inertia *(passivité),* in which the Quietists disregarded exterior works.

Fénelon's *Maximes* was doomed to failure. Cold, dry, boring, and basically ineloquent, it possesses all the charm of a mathematical treatise. Bossuet, predisposed, of course, to dislike the work, could scarcely have cared less about its defective method or its dogmatic exposition. What he saw in Fénelon's defense of pure love was not only an affirmation of many of the Guyonian principles, but a defiance of rational, logical Christianity. Unimpressed by Fénelon's saintly sources and impervious to his psychological nuances, he rejected Fénelon's concept of pure charity, which for him could not be separated within the soul from the idea of a beatifying God.[40] Unable, moreover, to comprehend his opponent's mystical condemnation of activity (not action), Bossuet refused to accept the doctrine of the passive state. His ripostes, beginning in March of 1697 with the successful *Instruction sur les états d'oraison (Instruction on the States of Prayer)*, followed later that year by such works as the *Mémoire* of July 15, 1697 and the *Sommaire de la doctrine du livre Explication des maximes des saints (Summary of the Doctrine of the Book Explanation of the Maxims of the Saints*, August, 1697), made it more than clear to Fénelon that he was dealing with a talented and wily adversary. Public opinion had quite obviously shifted to the side of the enemy; he knew that somehow he had to reassure his friends and save his book from papal censure.

V *The* Instruction pastorale *(September 15, 1697)*

Fénelon, despite his insistence that his doctrine was in no way heretical, soon found that he had rendered himself vulnerable on at least one very important point. Godet des Marais was among the first to claim that in the *Maximes* the concept of hope or *espérance*, one of the theological virtues, was considered an obstacle to perfection. Fénelon was aware that his explanation of self-interest *(intérêt propre)*, the specific motive of hope, could be construed in two different senses: it could be taken to mean the desired or hoped-for object of every Christian, or else it could be interpreted as the "egoistic incentive" *(mobile égoiste)* which induced the soul to hope. This latter notion clearly needed elucidation.

Fénelon's reply to the charges and the questions came in the form of a long treatise, a pastoral instruction dated September 15, 1697, written on the subject of hope. In reality it is his attempt to establish once and for all the boundaries that separate the fourth and fifth states or degrees of love. To do so, Fénelon must introduce a concept, not a new one, since, as he acknowledged, it is to be found in the work of many orthodox authors, notably Saint Bernard. This is "natural love," or as he also calls it, "a mercenary affection" (2, 290). This motive is not evil in itself; it is simply imperfect. As such, it diminishes the perfection of the will and therefore disappears almost completely in the fifth or most supreme state of love where charity takes precedence over hope. By using the term "natural love" Fénelon also seeks to prove that mystical indifference has no bearing on the soul's lack of concern for its salvation. Just as the soul can desire its happiness, so can it also reject the idea of "natural love." In doing so, the passive state in turn becomes the beneficiary, for now it is truly active and in no way attached through "worry or eagerness" (2, 298) to a mercenary self-love. In the summation to his *Instruction pastorale* Fénelon made clear still another point: that "pure love" is neither an impression, a sensation, nor a temporary act; it is an habitual state devoid of any variability.

Despite Bossuet's charges that Fénelon's introduction of "natural love" into the issue was only an ingenious invention designed to change or circumvent the issues at hand, this *Instruction* is possibly Fénelon's best defense.[41] Devised with more clarity and supported with better documentation than the *Maximes*, it develops to advantage some of the author's statements about imperfect love found in the *Explication des articles d'Issy* (for example, Articles XII and XXI) as well as his ideas concerning property which are part of the *Maximes* (Article XIV, for example). The encouraging news at this point was that the *Instruction pastorale* was well received in Rome where the cardinals and theologians were deciding the fate of the *Maximes*. For Fénelon it was a signal of victory, a sure sign that the enemy had at last been outmatched.

VI *Defeat and Condemnation*

Fénelon's optimism was short-lived. In early March, 1698, thanks to the machinations of Bossuet, there was a strong hint of scandal in the air. Father La Combe, a prisoner at Vincennes, was ready to admit that his relationship with Madame Guyon had been anything but pure. His confession, in the form of a letter, was duly produced, with the result that Fénelon and his friends were, on the basis of unsubstantiated facts, most gravely compromised. On June 2, 1698, Louis XIV exiled from the court, among others, two of the archbishop's closest associates, the Abbé Beaumont and the Abbé de Langeron. Not long afterwards Fénelon's brother was forced to resign his commission in the army.

Fénelon was to experience still another blow, which came in the form of Bossuet's *Relation sur le quiétisme (Report on Quietism)*, published on June 26, 1698. Written to demonstrate that the doctrine of the Archbishop of Cambrai was the same as Madame Guyon's, and that the tenets of the latter were no different from those of Molinos, Bossuet's work was more personal than theological. To enforce the verity of his accusations, Bossuet had used statements from Madame Guyon's manuscripts, confidentially entrusted to him. The result was a text which, cleverly exploiting the pious and volatile statements of Fénelon's friend, crushed the author of the *Moyen court* under the weight of buffoonery and ridicule. Fénelon, of course, fared no better. Bossuet attempts to show that Fénelon, through his blind adherence to her doctrines, authorized in no uncertain terms her madness. In disrespect for his former protegé, Bossuet goes so far as to refer to Fénelon as a Montanus defending his Priscilla.[42]

Bossuet's stinging irony and well-calculated persiflage did not go unappreciated. The *Relation* was an immense success, and once more Fénelon was pushed into a corner. His answer came in the form of the *Réponse à la Relation sur le quiétisme (Response to the Report on Quietism)* published in August, 1698. In comparison to Bossuet's *Relation* it is a calm, moderate, subtle statement. Fénelon neither repudiates nor censures Madame Guyon; he simply reminds his readers that if she is indeed a demon, then he and others (including the Bishop of Geneva) were deceived by a life that he always considered to be saintly and spiritual. Fénelon also retraces his version of the history of the Quietist quarrel, referring to Bossuet's breach of confidence and his violation of the confessional. The *Réponse à la Relation* may have been effective in restoring the public's confidence in Fénelon, but like its sequels—Bossuet's *Remarques sur la réponse de M. de Cambrai (Remarks on the Response of M. de Cambrai)* and Fénelon's *Réponse aux Remarques—(Response to the Remarks)*—it added nothing new, either doctrinally or otherwise, to the debate. The worst of it was, of course, that the two churchmen had become bitter enemies.

The judgment from Rome, when it was finally handed down that March of 1699, was not as decisive as Bossuet and Louis XIV had wanted. Although the papal brief used such adjectives as "rash," "scandalous," and "offensive" to describe the twenty-three propositions, the doctrine condemned can basically be reduced to two major points: (1) There are certain souls so submissive to God that if, in a state of tribulation, they were to believe that God had condemned them, they would sacrifice to Him, in an absolute manner, their salvation. (2) In this life there is a state of perfection in which there is no longer any reason to desire reward or to fear punishment.[43] The act of "pure love" was not mentioned, but the sentence passed against the *Maximes* underscored Rome's disapproval of the preeminence given by Fénelon to the contemplative life as opposed to the meditative and to the disappropriation of virtues.

Perhaps the greatest immediate effect of the condemnation of the *Maximes* was the restraining force that it exerted on what was no doubt the greatest mystical movement in seventeenth-century Europe. For some while to come—at least until fairly late in the eighteenth century—a cloud of suspicion and an atmosphere of repression would weigh upon Catholic mysticism. In his efforts to keep the Church within the bounds of a rational, bourgeois-like piety, Bossuet had at least momentarily emerged the victor. On the other hand, in another very significant way, Fénelon and Madame Guyon had opened the doors to a realm where instinct, imagination, and the illusions of the heart held sway; they had almost involuntarily prepared the way for the collapse of the old order and the triumph of the sentimental revolution.[44]

CHAPTER 5

Télémaque

I Background and Sources

IN a letter addressed to Father Le Tellier (1710), Fénelon tells us
about the form, the aim, and the sources of *Télémaque:* ". . . It is
a fabulous narrative in the form of a heroic poem, like those written
by Homer and Virgil, into which I incorporated the major lessons
suitable for a prince who by virtue of his birth is destined to reign
. . ." (7, 665). Even without this information, it is evident that Fénelon's romance is linked by spirit and inspiration to the Homeric
tradition. For one thing, the title of the first edition, *Suite du quatrième livre de l'Odysée d'Homère ou les Aventures de Télémaque,
fils d'Ulysse (Sequel to the Fourth Book of Homer's Odyssey or the
Adventures of Telemachus, Son of Ulysses)*, reveals his intention to
fashion his story into something of a sequel to Homer's epic poem, a
narrative which was designed to run parallel to those last adventures
that precede the return of Ulysses to Ithaca. Then, if we examine
the episodic structure, if we take note of certain descriptive details
(such as Telemachus' shield of Book XIII), the pictorial touches (the
dolphins of Book IV, for example), as well as the digressions concerning the characters' exploits and the use of intervening gods, we
become aware of how much Fénelon owes to the art and technique
of both Homer and Virgil. Finally, the didactic quality of *Télémaque*
suggests still another example of Fénelon's faithfulness to the concept that Homer, despite the coarseness of his pagan mores and
religion, was, as one of Fénelon's editors phrases it, "a useful
teacher of morals."[1]

It would be very deceptive, however, to confine the background
and sources of *Télémaque* to Homer and Virgil alone. For his evocation of the Mediterranean world and his recreation of a mythic and
moral universe, Fénelon turned to the work of a large number of
ancient authors: Xenophon's *Cyropaedia*, for example, influenced

perhaps as much as any other work the didactic quality of the romance, while Ovid's *Metamorphoses* provided Fénelon a rich fund from which to draw the mythological allusions. Historical and geographical details were supplied by Herodotus and Diodorus (the description of Egypt in Book II) as well as by Pliny the Elder, Titus Livy (information about Spain and Italy), and Strabo. As for Sophocles, we have only to recall the interpolated story of Philoctetes in Book XII to realize Fénelon's debt to that dramatist. To round out this catalogue, which is by no means complete, it would be necessary also to include Aristotle (The *Politics*, more specifically), Plato (The *Laws*), and Plutarch (his life of Lycurgus has a direct bearing on certain passages in Book V), whose influence is quite evident.[2]

Fénelon's great absorption of ancient letters should not hide from view the possibility that he assimilated still another type of literature, which in a way is related to the verse epic—that of the adventure novel of the earlier part of the seventeenth century. Those long, rambling novels, such as Gomberville's *Polexandre* (1637) and La Calprenède's *Cassandre* (1642–45), transported the reader through the peregrinations of the hero to faraway, marvellous, sometimes exotic lands. In most cases the author, reaching beyond the bounds of pure entertainment, felt obliged to furnish the reader a certain amount of didactic as well as pseudoscientific and historical material. Fénelon's attention to geographical detail, his belief in the Horatian concept of blending profit with delight (the *utile dulci*), and the narrative technique itself recall those characteristics. Closely allied to this particular novelistic form is the vogue for the imaginary voyage, a genre which began to achieve popularity in the last quarter of the seventeenth century. Rabelais' *Pantagruel* (1532) is an earlier manifestation of this tradition; but such works as Gabriel Foigny's *Les Aventures de Jacques Sadeur* (1672) and the anonymous *Histoire des Sévarambes* (1677), which features a voyage to a utopia, were probably known if not read by Fénelon.[3] At any rate, our preceptor was most certainly in tune to the tastes of the public, particularly a young public, for this sort of fiction; his earlier "Voyage dans l'Ile des Plaisirs" ("Voyage to Pleasure Island") as well as the "Voyage supposé en 1690" ("An Imaginary Trip in 1690") indicate that even before he began to compose *Télémaque* he was already fully aware of the appealing nature of travels and adventures in uncharted lands.

The works of other writers, too, contemporaries of Fénelon, must

certainly have affected his ideas. It would be impossible not to
mention again, for example, the Abbé Fleury (his *Moeurs des Is-
raélites* and *Pensées politiques (Political Thoughts)* seem particularly
influential), as well as Bossuet whose *Discours sur l'histoire universelle (Discourse on Universal History)* undoubtedly impressed
Fénelon. Finally,there is one last title worthy of mention, although
its influence on Fénelon is highly questionable. In 1609 a former
professor at the University of Paris, Petrus Valens (1561–1641),
published a third collection of discourses treating rhetorical con-
troversies called *Telemachus, sive de profectu in virtute et sapientia
(Telemachus, or Growth in Virtue and Knowledge)*. The title itself is
suggestive of Fénelon's work, but what is more noteworthy is Valens' inclusion of an exhortation addressed to Telemachus by
Minerva, who appears in the guise of Mentor.[4] For lack of other
information, we can only accept this as an interesting indication and
nothing more.

II *The Narrative*

As the story begins, the nymph Calypso, disconsolate still over
the departure of Ulysses from her island, espies the wreckage of a
ship and its two passengers who have managed to escape the fury of
the storm. Recognizing the younger of the two as Ulysses' son, she
welcomes the young man and his guide, who is none other than
Minerva disguised as Mentor. Calypso immediately conceives a passion for Telemachus; but the latter, having been warned by Mentor
of the dangers of a sybaritic life, spurns her offers for immortality
and a life of ease. She casts aside her amorous intentions—at least
for the moment—and asks that Telemachus tell her of his adventures since the time he left Ithaca in search of his father. He then
recounts his trip to Pylos and Lacedemonia, his shipwreck on the
coast of Sicily, and his experience in battle against the enemies of
Acestes, king of that island. He continues his narrative by describing his enslavement in Egypt, his encounter there of Termosiris,
who initiates him into the cult for Apollo, and his meeting with the
benevolent King Sesostris. The latter's sudden demise again spells
misfortune for Telemachus, for he is imprisoned in a tower by Bocchoris, the evil son of Sesostris. After a battle between Bocchoris'
troops and a force of rebels aided by the Phoenicians, in which the
malevolent ruler perishes, Telemachus is liberated by the insur-
gents and carried off to Tyr, capital of Phoenicia.

Here, barely escaping death at the hands of the tyrant Pygmalion, he flees to Cyprus, an island dedicated to Venus and the joys of sensual pleasure. Telemachus, close to falling prey to the idle, voluptuous life of the Cyprians, is saved by Mentor who now reappears (he had been enslaved in Ethiopia at the time of Telemachus's Egyptian bondage). Together with Hasael, Mentor's new master, they leave for Crete. Here they are able to observe the courageous, healthy, peace-loving inhabitants and learn of their late king, Minos, a ruler whose administration had been dedicated to the well-being and prosperity of his subjects. Telemachus is admitted to the assembly appointed to choose a new king; he participates in the athletic games, winning several prizes, and impresses the elders with his answers to their political and moral questions. When they decide to elect him king, he graciously declines, embarking once more upon his quest for his father. It is at this point in the story that a shipwreck, the product of Venus' anger, casts him upon Calypso's island.

Having concluded the recital of his adventures, Telemachus is urged by Mentor to take his leave of Calypso and her nymphs. The young man, however, has succumbed to the power of Venus who is still anxious to claim him as a victim. The object of his love is not Calypso, but one of her nymphs, Eucharis. In order to combat this passion, which Telemachus himself cannot overcome, Mentor devises a plan: by revealing to Calypso Telemachus's newfound love he will be able to incite her jealousy and thus secure her aid in arranging their departure. The stratagem is successful, for the angry Calypso not only suggests that Mentor construct a ship, but with fiery words she banishes Telemachus from her kingdom. As he and Mentor prepare to board their vessel, Cupid appears and persuades the nymphs to burn the craft. For a fleeting moment Telemachus rejoices at the sight of the flames; Mentor, however, forcibly directs him toward the open sea, and the two swim out to a Phoenician ship which is anchored near the island. They are welcomed on board by Adoam, the commander, who promises to take Telemachus to Ithaca. In the course of their voyage, Adoam relates for them the tragic death of Pygmalion and describes his visit to Baetica (La Bétique), a country, marvellous in climate and resources, whose inhabitants are guided by the principles of industry and simplicity. At the conclusion of this narrative, the voyagers, unaware that they have been tricked by Neptune, discover that they have landed, not at Ithaca, but at Salentum, a kingdom recently established by Idomeneus, the grandson of Minos.

The sojourn in Salentum affords Mentor the occasion to advise Idomeneus concerning the organization and administration of his country. Telemachus' guide becomes, in fact, the architect of a series of social, political, and economic reforms designed to ensure the well-being of the state: after negotiating a peace settlement between Idomeneus and his neighbors the Mandurians, he demonstrates for that king how he should both regulate and stimulate commerce; he persuades him to encourage the cultivation of useful arts, to ban the manufacture of luxury items, and to promote agricultural development. Mentor also provides Idomeneus with a plan for dividing the citizens into seven distinct classes. From the moral standpoint he convinces the king that he should recall from exile the virtuous Philocles who had been slandered and betrayed by the treacherous Protésilas.

While Mentor is engaged in the reconstruction and reform of Salentum, Telemachus joins the army of Idomeneus' allies and leaves to fight the Daunians. He wins the respect of the older leaders, even Philoctetes, who despite his former animosity for Ulysses, counsels his new friend on the dangers of love and relates to him his tribulations and adventures during the era of the Trojan war. Not all those among the allied forces, however, are favorably disposed toward the young warrior. When Phalantes, the Lacedemonian general, and Hippias, his brother, challenge his right to certain Daunian prisoners, Telemachus, in a fit of uncontrolled anger, engages the latter in combat. Although he is able to subdue Hippias, Telemachus, ashamed of his lack of self-control, retreats to his quarters, leaving the camp quarrelsome and divided over the internal altercation. At this point Adraste, the enemy king, takes advantage of the dissension to launch a surprise attack. Telemachus rallies the troops and saves the army from complete destruction; he further redeems himself for his past conduct by personally overseeing the funeral service for Hippias, one of the casualties of the near-disastrous battle.

With calm and order restored to the allied forces, Telemachus steals from the camp during the night to embark on a new mission. Having been convinced by a series of dreams that his father is no longer alive, he feels compelled to learn the truth by visiting the underworld, the entrance to which he locates in the famous cavern of Acherontia. Pluto permits him to visit both areas of Hades—Tartarus where he observes the torments of, among others, the tyrannical, selfish, negligent monarchs; and the Elysian Fields, where he learns of the reward reserved for all the earth's good and just kings. It is here among the virtuous that Telemachus is recognized by Arcesius, his great-grandfather, who informs him that Ulysses is alive and will soon return to Ithaca. After receiving a lesson in the art of kingship from his ancestor, Telemachus returns to earth and resumes his duties with the allied troops. He participates in one last battle against the Daunians, slays Adrastes, and becomes instrumental in effecting a fair and humane peace settlement.

His military career ended, Telemachus returns to Salentum where he is able to note the final effects of Mentor's transformation of Idomeneus' kingdom. Also in this last phase of the narrative the protagonist finds in the person of Antiope, Idomeneus' daughter, a woman who is worthy of a future sovereign. His marriage to her must be deferred, however, until his mission is accomplished and he can secure his father's approval. Telemachus and Mentor thus take leave of Idomeneus, who is reluctant to have them go. In the course of the voyage (still another break in the action which gives Mentor the opportunity to give his pupil further instructions concerning the principles of kingship), their ship is becalmed and they must land on an uncharted island. Here Telemachus encounters a stranger whom he does not recognize as his father, but whose presence and attitude emotionally affect him. Mentor consoles him by finally revealing Ulysses' identity and by assuring him that this final test of patience is only a prelude to the reuniting of father and son. Shortly thereafter, Mentor reassumes the form of Minerva, gives her pupil some last instructions, and disappears in a golden-azure cloud. The astonished Telemachus, making a hasty departure, reaches Ithaca where he finds his father in the company of Eumaeus.

III *The Moral Lesson*

Even though *Télémaque*, like the *Fables* and the *Dialogues des morts*, is faithful to the precepts of Fénelon's indirect instruction, it is a work marked by a "more noble tone" and a "more sustained seriousness" than those earlier works.[5] The grave inflection of this romance can be explained in part by the fact that the reader, no matter how intensely he may be absorbed by the color and excitement of the ancient world, is never allowed to forget that this is the story of one long moral and spiritual odyssey. *Télémaque* also possesses a greater singleness of thought and purpose than Fénelon's other fictional creations, not only by virtue of its form, but also because of the unifying force that is derived from the presence of Mentor. This is not to say that the goddess Minerva, transformed into human shape, is the author's only spokesman for his program of edification. Other characters—Termosiris, Philoctetes, Arcesius, even Telemachus, for example—perform on occasion that role, but it is Mentor who unquestionably guides and directs Telemachus toward a gradual moral victory.

IV *Simplicity, Naturalness, and the Innocent Life*

By the time Fénelon turned to the composition of *Télémaque*, he had clearly established himself as a proponent of the natural and as an enemy of artifice and affectation. While the *Dialogues sur l'éloquence* applied his canon of simplicity primarily to artistic and literary matters, the *Éducation des filles*, the *Fables*, and to some degree the *Dialogues des morts*, sought to relate those principles to human mores and conduct. In *Télémaque* we see no less a reaffirmation of his values, except that here Fénelon concentrates, with a greater emphasis than in the *Fables*, on equating naturalness with the benefits of a sober, moderate life set against the background of external nature itself.

For Fénelon the greatest stumbling block to man's achievement of the ideal existence is his attachment to the vain and materialistic trappings of society. Part of the utopian scheme of *Télémaque* is to demonstrate to the hero that luxury, ostentation, and the soft, vigorless quality of one's moral fiber (*luxe, faste,* and *mollesse*—those nouns that occur with such frequency throughout the narrative) are pitfalls along the road that leads to the achievement of true honor and probity. Long before Fénelon turns his attention to Mentor's reforms at Salentum, he has clearly pointed out, both in his description of Cretan society (Book V) and in his portrait of idyllic La Bétique (Book VII), that the "superfluous" items of daily life are really quite unnecessary. Expensive clothing, rich furnishings, and all such goods associated with the pursuit of wealth, are responsible in the main for man's ambitious drive, his avarice, and his fears.

Since Fénelon more than implies that wisdom comes by studying "simple nature" (6, 452), it is not surprising to note the great emphasis that he places on agriculture and the happy drama of human life played out against a backdrop of cultivated fields and lowing cattle. Although his attitude is most certainly motivated by the real economic and social conditions of his era (the vast stretches of untended land in France, the great famine of 1693–94, for example), Fénelon seeks a solution to moral woes in the sober diet and the hard work of those devoted to tilling the soil. So it is that Telemachus is charmed at the sight of Egypt's fertile land, the fruitful gardens at Tyre, and the flowering countryside of Salentum. In *Télémaque* the beauty and prosperity of field and furrow are very much the symbols of moral regeneration; the return to nature—a flight to innocence, as it were—brings with it, as in "Les Aventures de Mélésichthon" (Fable XXXV) the reward of virtue, health, peace, and happiness.

V *The Uses of Adversity*

Telemachus, whose exploits are marked by definite personal achievements (the athletic games of Book V and victory on the battlefield in Book XV, for example), experiences, nonetheless, a number of setbacks in the course of Fénelon's story. These reversals of fortune, as Mentor reminds him on more than one occasion (Books II, VI, and VIII), are designed not to destroy him, but rather to strengthen his character and prepare him for a future of esteem and honor. During his captivity in Egypt, sad and despairing, Telemachus hears the voice of his tutelary goddess (or so he believes) urging him to be patient. Suffering and misfortune, he is told, will only teach him to comfort others. As a future ruler he will then be aware of how important it is to love his subjects and assuage their griefs. In Book VIII, when Adoam's ship is blown off course by Neptune and the disheartened Telemachus bemoans his fate, he is reminded by Mentor that anyone who does not know how to suffer does not possess greatness of heart. To triumph over cruel fortune he must have patience and courage. Later, in Book XII, Telemachus hears something of a variation of this moral concept as Philoctetes proclaims to Neoptolemus: "Those who have never suffered know nothing; they are unacquainted with either good or evil; they do not know men; they do not know themselves" (6, 501).

The lessons of Mentor and Philoctetes on the uses of adversity (they recall Henri IV's statement to the Duc de Mayenne in Dialogue LXIX) prove to be effective. In the wake of Telemachus' moral regeneration ("quick" and "astonishing," it might appear),[6] which is evident after Book XIII, he finds use for that wise counsel. Introduced in Book XVI to Diomedes, the Aetolian king who became the victim of Venus' wrath after wounding her at the siege of Troy, Telemachus is quickly able to relate that man's separation from homeland and family to his own. In words that echo his earlier instruction, he tells Diomedes that through suffering one learns to be compassionate. Then he states: "Misfortune adds a new luster to the reputation of great men; they lack something if they have never known the meaning of unhappiness" (6, 543).

VI   Patriotic Love and Fidelity

In Book XVI, Telemachus is offered, as part of his reward in the victory over the Daunians, the region of Arpinum. A land rich in farmland, vineyards, and olive groves, it proves, however, no temptation for our protagonist. Without hesitation he proclaims his love for Ithaca, despite its huts, its "frightful crags," and "savage woods" (6, 541). Unaffected by the temptation of territorial expansion and wary of the idea of ruling people who might very well be "intractable, restless, unjust, deceptive, and ungrateful" (6, 542), he clearly states his intention to return to his parents and homeland. It is there that one day he hopes to reign with "justice, piety, and courage" (6, 542). Telemachus' patriotic and unselfish attitude reflects the virtuous stance of Furius Camillus, who in the *Dialogue des morts* (XXXIV) tells Marcus Coriolanus that even when a person is far from his country, he should "respect her, wish for her the best, be ready to return there prepared to defend and die for her" (6, 278).

VII   Flattery and Praise

Fénelon's revelation of the pernicious effects of flattery in *Télémaque* is carried out with an even greater illustrative power and psychological intensity than in the *Dialogues des morts*. Not only is the reader provided, for example, the well-developed portrait of Idomeneus, a man who has become inured to flattery, but also the incisive, rather pathetic image of Nestor, who in his declining years succumbs to vain and treacherous praise and reveals military secrets.

Telemachus himself is no stranger to this serious moral defect, given the fact that he had been "flattered by his mother since infancy" (6, 504). By the time we reach Book XVI, however, he is seemingly immune to the harmful consequences of flattery. He is reluctant and embarrassed to accept the compliments and plaudits of the allied leaders, preferring instead to give them his view of how dangerous praise can be: "It is not," he says, "that I dislike it, particularly when it comes from such good judges of virtue; but the fact is that I am afraid of liking it too much" (6, 541). Praise, he continues, corrupts men, causing them to become vain and presumptuous; therefore, it must be merited but avoided, for even the best of it resembles the worst. The sort of praise to be preferred is that given to a person in his absence.

Telemachus' moral stricture concerning flattery would seemingly imply that he is sufficiently on his guard; but Mentor, in his last instruction to the hero in Book XVIII, finds it necessary to speak of it again. His comments are not entirely repetitious, since he chooses to relate the psychology of praise to cause rather than to effect. As he explains to his charge, there are certain rulers who do not know the meaning of true virtue. Something about it is "too austere and independent," something which in the final analysis "frightens and embitters" them (6, 558). Caught in this predicament, they turn to flattery, at which point they become incapable of finding either sincerity or virtue. The result is, of course, disastrous: the sovereign learns to trust no one, and in doing so becomes jealous, fearful and—what is worse—inaccessible.

VIII *The Three Faces of Love*

An essential part of both the moral program and the novelistic interest of *Télémaque* is Fénelon's revelation of the deceptive, misleading—even deadly—aspects of love. Even if he had confined himself to a description of Deianira's undoing of Hercules (Book XII) or to the story of Astarbé's unsavory machinations (Book III), the preceptor might well have made his point. Not content, however, to relegate his exploration of a primary passion to any sort of secondary level, he chooses to accentuate its fictional dimension by having Telemachus personally experience first the tortuous, disordered effects of love, and later, almost at the end of the story, its reasonable and serene capacity.

By the time Telemachus reaches Calypso's island, he is no stranger to the force of Venus' power. His near-escape from the idle, dissolute love-cult at Cythera in Book IV has made him, it would seem, all the more vulnerable to the seductive charm of Calypso.

The young man is indeed attracted by the fiery, almost-dazzling quality of her beauty; but under the watchful eye of Mentor, who rather constantly reminds him (in Books I and IV) of the danger of "the hidden poison" of her gentle, flattering words, the "unctuous poison of her praise," he remains impassive and, in her estimation, disarmingly aloof (6, 400; 420). By the time we reach Book VI, Calypso is no longer the lovely, incandescent creature of the earlier sections; she has become aware that the sweetness and the mildness that have so greatly tempered her passion are ineffective. It is at this point that she resorts to a psycho-erotic device. By placing Telemachus in close contact with the most beautiful of her nymphs, she hopes to awaken the fires of his love. Calypso is seconded in her attempt by the intervention of Venus and by the very direct presence of Cupid. Cradled and petted by the nymphs, coddled by an unwary Telemachus, the "mocking and wicked" little Eros wreaks his havoc: the hero is turned into a simpering, languishing victim who falls in love with the nymph Eucharis; and Calypso, once the proud Dido-like figure of the story, is transformed into a Racinian Hermione, a fury of a woman (an "infernal fury" as Mentor calls her) rendered half-mad by jealousy and passion.[7]

So it is that the center of attention is shifted, at least for a brief interlude, to Eucharis. Although Fénelon leaves the reader with the impression that she is a younger Calypso, a *jeune fille* who has yet to experience the disenchantments and heartbreak of love, he wastes but few words in describing her. Her delineation totally lacks that progressive psychological development that marks the author's portrait of Calypso. It is somewhat surprising that at least seven eighteenth-century artists, in creating scenes from *Télémaque* for the various *salons*, selected Eucharis as the visual idealization of Telemachus' love. Perhaps it is her pathetic role of abandoned woman that attracted not only certain painters, but also such people as Houdard de La Motte and Madame Roland who were enchanted and moved by the Eucharis episode.[8] Fénelon would have been, no doubt, disappointed if not alarmed at this reaction. There is indeed about Eucharis a certain aura of innocence, but she is nonetheless unworthy of the young man. Her action in the narrative is marked by Fénelon's use of the words "artifice" and "artificial"; even when she appears in the hunting episode dressed as the goddess Diana, the reader is apt to sense the author's ironic touch. In short, Eucharis' more appealing qualities are negated by her use of feminine wiles and by the falseness of her charm.

Telemachus' escape from the clutches of Calypso and Eucharis, choreographed and directed by Mentor-Minerva, represents more than just an adventurous escapade: it is a symbolic retreat from the realm of violent passion to a land where reason and wisdom hold sway. The author's condemnation of love in the early episodes of *Télémaque* is directed not against love itself, but against the blinding, disturbing, harmful effects of ardent, impassioned love. For Telemachus it is a luxury he cannot afford, since in the eyes of Fénelon the surrender to such profligacy is tantamount to the renouncement of family, duty, and a future which holds great promise. Action, heroism, accomplishment are part of the hero's (also a future king's) ethic; Telemachus' romantic destiny lies in wait on calmer shores, where the feminine ideal is synonymous with order and equilibrium.

Not until near the end of his adventures, on his return to Salentum, does Telemachus find the feminine representative of propriety and sagacity. Quite suddenly he announces to Mentor that he loves Antiope, Idomeneus' daughter, and almost in the same breath declares that it is not "a blind passion" (6, 550). He admits that he has been deeply wounded by love, that time and absence have not completely healed him; but that in Antiope he has found the perfect future wife. His catalogue of her virtues, as well as Mentor's words of praise, which to a large extent echo those of the young man, recall to the reader the pages of the *Éducation des filles* where Fénelon extols a young woman's modesty, industry, domestic efficiency, simpleness in dress and ornamentation, and amiable temperament.[9] Antiope thus becomes Fénelon's fictionalized embodiment of the ideal companion, a composite of Diana and Minerva (to whom she is actually compared) and therefore nothing less than a paragon of wisdom and virtue. When Telemachus is told that he must wait to claim her as his bride, he voices no objection; in the words of Fénelon, "He was no longer the same Telemachus who had formerly been captivated by a tyrannical passion on Calypso's isle" (6, 553). Reason has taken the upper hand over feeling, and the hero's love story ends not in a tragic or dramatic way but with the triumph of sense over sensibility, the victory of love directed by Christian psychology over sensual domination.[10]

IX *The Religious Element*

It might seem at first glance, given its ancient cadre and its fictional manipulation of a world of gods and heroes, that a work such as *Télémaque* would be incapable of fusing pagan wisdom and Christianity. Although it is true that Fénelon avoids introducing objectively any specific Christian element, he does, on the other hand, present us a Homeric Greece, that expresses in a subtle and complex fashion the mysticism of its author.[11]

This process of "spiritualization" in *Télémaque*, although not completely indifferent to concrete, objective, Christian-inspired precepts (the fundamental importance of peace, fear of the gods, the concept of a brotherhood of men, for example), is one which in the final analysis emphasized the achievement of virtue and wisdom through an interior peace and happiness. Fénelon's view of heaven (the Elysian Fields) in Book XIV is, to use the critic Jules Lemaître's phrase, that of "a paradise of mystics lost in God, scarcely distinct from Him."[12] Here the souls are fed on a pure light, "a celestial glory," which, having penetrated their bodies, plunges them into an "abyss of joy, like fish in the sea" (6, 524). It is this purity, capable of satisfying their desires and filling their souls with serenity, that "lifts them above everything that shallow and voracious men seek on earth" (6, 524–25). The "torrent of divinity," flowing endlessly through their hearts is Fénelon's mystic stream, a spontaneous emanation sent by the Supreme Power to guide man toward perfection. It well may be that at the time Fénelon wrote *Télémaque* his mysticism was oriented toward the contemplative life and centered about the peace, calm, and rest with which the soul is capable of being flooded.[13]

In the course of his visit to the underworld, Telemachus discovers another image of light which is also related to Fénelon's moral and theological credo. Led by Minos among the tormented souls of Tartarus, the protagonist encounters an unnamed philosopher who during his life on earth had been virtuous and dutiful toward his fellow man. What the philosopher is guilty of, as Minos explains, is the appropriation of his own virtue. Shutting himself away within the confines of his own good deeds and ignoring the gods, he had relied on his self-esteem to the point that he became his own divinity. The punishment for this pride, as Telemachus learns, takes the form of an "obtrusive light" which constantly pursues him everywhere; nowhere is he safe from "the piercing rays of truth . . . which he has neglected to follow" (6, 522). Fénelon's lesson in humility is related in a diffused fashion to his concept of grace, but perhaps more importantly to his theological view of "property," one type of which as defined in the *Maximes des saints* is a love of one's own excellence "devoid of any subordination to our essential end which is the glory of God."[14] This brand of pride is but another stumbling block to the achievement of the ideal, another barrier to man's harmony and peace.

X The Political Message: The Two Utopias

European literature and thought, beginning with Thomas More in the sixteenth century and continuing on into the twentieth with the work of Teilhard de Chardin, have produced a rather long succession of utopias. In *Télémaque* we find one of the first French attempts to transform "the Morean image of a society free of private property, avarice, and ambition into a land of calm felicity where the complex troubles of civilization vanished."[15]

Fénelon's fantasy actually embraces two major utopias, and it is the first of these, La Bétique, which is responsible for that serene, Edenic conversion mentioned above. Like the idealized landscapes and communities found in Fénelon's pastoral fables, it recalls, in an almost nostalgic fashion, the Golden Age of man's existence. La Bétique (geographically it suggests Andalucia in southern Spain) is portrayed as a primitivistic, agrarian, nomadic society whose inhabitants, "simple and happy in their simplicity" (6, 451), scorn the wealth, sophistication, and commerce of other nations. Ruled by fraternal love and egalitarian principles, they are content to live off the land in a sort of rustic communism; interested neither in money nor in territorial expansion, they represent the qualities of peace, liberty, and innocence.

Since Mentor and Telemachus only hear about and never visit La Bétique, it remains for them, as for the reader, only an idyllic vision. Although an excellent lesson, intended, as George Havens suggests, "to wean his royal pupil from attachment to court luxury and the engrossing complexities of modern life," this example of a back-to-nature society is too idealistic for Fénelon.[16] Like Plato, who in the second book of *The Republic* creates a communistic, naturalistic utopia and then later rejects it in favor of an alternate state, Fénelon directs his efforts toward more practical goals. In his reconstruction of Salentum, where he does not allow himself to be dazzled by poetic suppositions, he achieves the creation of government and a society that he sincerely hoped could be realized in France.[17]

Mentor's first sweeping measures of reform are designed to make Idomeneus' kingdom a powerful commercial state. Unlike Louis XIV's minister Colbert, he advises that freedom and fluidity in trade become the initial steps toward assuring the prosperity of a nation. Maritime supervision and regulation are necessary, as are laws dealing with bankruptcy; but commerce, he points out, must not be impeded by taxes which only tend to repel rather than attract trade. Fénelon's idea of economic success, based on a sound import-export system, foreshadows Voltaire's later view concerning the benefits of commerce in the *Lettres philosophiques* (*Philosophical Letters*, 1734).

Commerce is not to be the only source of prosperity for Salentum. In his scheme of things, Mentor envisions a society that is to be founded on sound agrarian principles. Viewing the vast stretches of fertile but fallow land, he counsels Idomeneus on ways to improve productivity. For one thing, he advocates the transferal of unneeded artisans and workers from the city to the country, where, in a salubrious atmosphere, they will be able to ensure not only their well-being but to increase the agricultural yield. Mentor also proposes that those families who faithfully cultivate their land be rewarded with certain "favors and exemptions," while those guilty of neglect be subjected to fines and taxes (6, 482).

Fénelon's ideal state is, therefore, one that unquestionably embraces the work ethic; at the same time it lays great stress on "frugality and moderation" (6, 480). Under Mentor's guidance, Salentum becomes a very regimented political unit: luxury imports are forbidden, for example; the wearing of gold and silver ornaments proscribed. In addition, the government is to control such matters as diet (moderate and sober), architecture (simple and gracious, except for the temples), music (limited to the religious genre), and home furnishings (practical). The educational system, too, is to be administered by the state through a system of public schools "in which fear of the gods, love for country, respect for laws, and a preference for honor over pleasure and life itself" are taught (6, 482–83). Salentum, despite its restrictive, Draconian, and hierarchical depiction stands as Fénelon's tribute to the well-ordered state. It represents his reaction against Louis XIV's ineffective, dangerous principles of domestic policy, which, as he more than gently implies, were protected by nothing more than a deceptive semblance of glory and magnificence.

XI *War and Peace*

Télémaque bristles with the imagery and reality of war. The graphic, detailed battle scenes, particularly those of Books XIII and XV, while designed no doubt to furnish the reader a certain degree of entertainment, also acquaint Telemachus through both direct observation and vigorous participation with the meaningless horror of one of man's most barbarous activities. Telemachus' feat of arms may very well serve to add to his heroic luster; but, eventually, it leads him, amidst the carnage and bloodshed of Book XIII to the emotional realization that man's bellicose nature is motivated by an almost inexplicable rage, a "blind fury" (6, 513). He becomes aware that in many cases the desire for conquest originates in the mind of a ruler who is spurred on by vanity and the hope of achieving "a false glory" (6, 513). Wars, Telemachus decides, must be just ones, waged for the public good. More often than not, however, a prince may through unwise advice and jealousy lead his people into a conflict that is as harmful to them as to their enemies. By the time we reach Book XVII, Telemachus' disenchantment on the subject of war is complete. Sententiously declaring to Mentor that success in war "is always an odious and deadly thing" (6, 548), he also rhetorically asks why men do not prefer to seek honor and esteem in the performance of good works.

Telemachus' observations and conclusions concerning war, although the fruit of practical experience, are for the most part little more than an echo of his counselor's attitude. Mentor's first task upon his arrival in Salentum is to serve as mediator between the Hesperians, basically a warlike people, and the Mandurians, who are essentially peace-loving. In his advice to Idomeneus and his potential foes, he emphasizes the notion (repeated by Telemachus in Book XIII) that "all men are brothers," and that war, the "shame of mankind," should not be the instrument of a ruler's search for fame. Later on (in Books X and XI), in the midst of his instructions to Idomeneus Mentor returns to the subject of war, describing for him the disastrous effects of armed conflict on a nation, whether it be the aggressor or not. War, Mentor reminds him, drains a country of its strength; it is a great hindrance to commerce as well as agriculture, and, what is worse, "The best laws are weakened and the mores of the people are left to corruption" (6, 496).

Although Mentor, the incarnation of wisdom and virtue, is largely responsible for making *Télémaque* "the novel of peace,"[18] he does not refrain from telling his young charge that his courage must never be a dubious quality. "A prince," he informs Telemachus, "dishonors himself even more by avoiding the dangers of combat than by never going to war" (6, 475). Fénelon thus demonstrates his awareness that conciliation can never be the complete answer to a king's search for peace. When all else has failed, including the enlightened plan for a confederation or league of nations which he has Mentor suggest in Book IX, then sovereign and subjects must summon forth all the necessary valor and courage in support of a just and honorable cause.

XII   *The King*

Télémaque is virtually one long lesson in the art of kingship. In over half of its eighteen books, the protagonist is exposed, either through direct instruction or firsthand observance, to those principles that should guide any wise and virtuous monarch. Many of the precepts are reiterative of those already expounded in the *Dialogues des morts:* the necessity that a king love his subjects and that his energy be expended in the pursuit of their welfare; that he be surrounded by capable, sincere advisors; that he be immune to flattery, and that he set an example for simple, unostentatious living. *Télémaque* paints, as do the *Dialogues,* though perhaps with bolder, more colorful strokes, the portrait of the evil king. Pygmalion, the treacherous, bloodthirsty ruler of Phoenicia in Book III, is no doubt the best-remembered addition to Fénelon's catalogue of despotic and greedy monarchs. Ruled by hatred, he is a man who is ultimately carried to destruction by dint of his own fear and loneliness. Like Louis XI of the *Dialogues,* he is a fitting reminder to a young prince that the fruits of tyranny are bitter ones indeed.

Despite its similarity in matters of kingship to the *Dialogues,* *Télémaque* is in its way a more well-developed guidebook for rulers. This characteristic is borne out, for example, by Fénelon's rather extensive consideration of royal authority and absolutism. With great care he presents his case for monarchy that is to be devoid of arbitrary power. A king cannot act as if he alone were the state, for, as Mentor tells Idomeneus: "You are king only inasmuch as you have people to govern; and that your power must be measured, not by the extent of the lands which you occupy, but by the number of men who will inhabit these lands" (6, 473–74). It is also among his subjects that a ruler will find wise and reliable counselors, those who will help him to rule. "The more people a king has to rule," Telemachus is informed in Book X, "the more ministers he will need to carry out the work he cannot do by himself" (6, 476). In the final analysis, however, the king's authority rests on one great principle: that of the law. "Properly speaking," Mentor reminds Telemachus near the end of their adventures, "he [the King] defends the laws so that they might reign; he must be vigilant and hard-working in order to maintain them" (6, 561). As such, the sovereign is the least free and the least tranquil of anyone in the kingdom; he is really a slave "who sacrifices his rest and his liberty for freedom and the public good" (6, 561).

Kingship, as Mentor portrays it, is therefore an exigent, burden-some task. In no way does he try to hide its unattractive features; rather he attempts to show Telemachus that he cannot expect the impossible. Ruling a kingdom brings out the best as well as the worst in a man; and everything considered, no matter how good and wise he may be, he is still a man. Those in high places, Mentor concludes, are almost always subjected to a magnifying-glass sort of scrutiny. Given the fact that a king is never infallible, even though he be enlightened and virtuous, he deserves a certain amount of pity for having to rule "this innumerable multitude of corrupt and deceitful men" (6, 477).

XIII *The Impact and Influence of* Télémaque

The great public clamor, the almost incredible brouhaha of inter-est and outrage that greeted the publication of *Télémaque* quickly turned it into nothing more or less than a *succès de scandale*. Those who were not either delighted or incensed by what they recognized as a personal and harsh critique of Louis XIV's reign (Fénelon, of course, denied this) were content to see the romance as one long sort of scandal sheet, a deviously and carefully plotted *roman à clef*. So it is that many of Fénelon's contemporaries, guided and influenced at least in part by Guedeville's *Critique générale des Aventures de Télémaque* (*General Critique of the Adventures of Telemachus*, 1700), played about with the numerous possibilities of character identification: Mentor was most certainly Fénelon, and Telemachus the Duc de Bourgogne; Idomeneus was Louis XIV, unless, that is, the reader preferred to think of him as Pygmalion, who might also possibly represent Oliver Cromwell. Then there was

the wicked Astarbé, who, some were convinced, was either
Madame de Montespan, the king's former mistress, or perhaps
Madame de Maintenon.[19] With these names the list, of course, does
not end; for once the game had started, there was no end to its
various combinations and its clever discoveries.

Other contemporaries of Fénelon, chiefly those in theological
circles, were prepared to examine the work quite differently. Bossuet is reported to have found *Télémaque*'s amorous discourses and
gallant descriptions unworthy of a prelate.[20] Another churchman,
the Jansenist Faydit, produced a trenchant critique entitled *La
Télémacomanie* (*Telemacomania*, 1700) in which he declared that
the work was more dangerous than the *Maximes des saints*. Expressing his disdain for the fact that Fénelon had fallen into the "lower
depths" reserved for those who composed novels, he denounced the
"blasphemous" aspect of its mythology.[21] Seemingly ignoring the
moral and political significance of *Télémaque*, Faydit also concentrated on pointing out the anachronisms, the historical mistakes,
and the lack of judgment to be found in certain metaphysical expressions. The reaction of the great seventeenth-century critic Nicolas
Boileau, although not indicative of religious factions, represents no
doubt the impression of a certain number of contemporary critics:
admitting that *Télémaque* was capable of stimulating interest in *The
Odyssey*, he expressed the wish, however, that "the moral element
had been a little less imperceptibly prevalent."[22]

Such evaluations as those cited had absolutely no effect on the
popularity of *Télémaque*. Besides the more or less complete sixteen
editions which appeared in 1699, sixteen others were published
between 1700 and 1712. Beginning in 1701 with Granchamp's *Télémaque moderne*, there also began to appear a succession of imita-
tions—operas, lyric tragedies, and parodies (besides Marivaux's
Télémaque travesti, Lesage wrote one for the Saint-Germain Fair in
1715). With the publication in 1717 of the new and revised edition of
Télémaque by Fénelon's great-nephew, the Marquis de Fénelon,
(containing the glowing praise of Ramsay's *Discours sur la poésie
épique*) the cult for the Archbishop of Cambrai—which would be
based in large part on the public's knowledge of *Télémaque*—was,
one might say, initiated. By 1830 the number of editions would
swell to a total of 150, and that figure does not take into account the
some eighty translations produced during that period.[23]

Télémaque's influence on the eighteenth century cannot obviously be measured simply in terms of how many editions were

published. Far more important was its moral and political effect on writers of pre-Enlightenment and the Enlightenment proper. One of France's best-known eighteenth-century writers Montesquieu, for example, spoke of it as a "divine work," one "in which Homer seems to breathe."[24] Not only was he influenced by the literary qualities of *Télémaque* (its "enchanting" prose, for example), but by the political views as well. The troglodytes of Montesquieu's *Lettres persanes (Persian Letters)* of 1721 recall those noble savages of La Bétique, and his views on the efficacity of laws in *L'Esprit des lois (The Spirit of the Laws)* indicate that he must surely have carefully studied Fénelon's romance. Another guiding force of the Enlightenment, Voltaire, despite his cautious attitude toward Fénelon (he did not consider *Télémaque* a masterpiece), did not remain uninfluenced.[25] In 1736 he may well have chosen in his philosophical poem "Le Mondain" to parody "Monsieur du Télémaque" and the effects of abstemious living; but later, particularly in his philosophical tales *Zadig* (1749) and in *Micromégas* (1752), where he borrows Fénelon's epithet referring to the earth as a "heap of mud," we can discern why it is possible to look on *Télémaque* as an unmistakable forerunner of the eighteenth-century philosophical tale. Capable of being absorbed and modified by many spirits of the new reform, it grew to be the favorite text of a liberal and tolerant age. Up to the time of the Revolution, *Télémaque* continued to be read assiduously, either alluded to, or quoted by a galaxy of political and literary figures including Madame de Genlis, Condorcet, Robespierre, and Saint-Just.[26]

Probably just as important as the moral and political significance of *Télémaque* was the impact of its harmonious prose, its sensitive call to nature on those writers we usually term pre-Romantic. In particular, Jean-Jacques Rousseau, Bernardin de Saint-Pierre, and the pre-Romantic Chateaubriand—all of whom attest to their attraction for the work—must be cited as the inheritors of Fénelon's talent for descriptive passages and picturesque details. Theirs was a generation which, responding not only to the enthusiasm for humanitarian ideals and the appeal of primitive tableaux, also found affinity with the emotional effect of certain of Fénelon's scenes.[27] Narbal, Nestor, Diomedes, Idomeneus, and Telemachus are willing to shed an abundance of tears; the heart triumphant over restraint and reserve thus claims the allegiance of those kindred spirits who serve the cause of sensitivity and beneficence.

With the development of the novel in the nineteenth century and

the growth of a new scientific spirit, *Télémaque* came to be read less
and less. Even as a pedagogical manual or as a preferred book for
young people, it gradually lost its reputation. Today it is still
read—in France as well as abroad—but, from what I have been able
to determine, mostly in the form of excerpts. *Télémaque*, with its
"flowing, measured expression which makes of it an elegant pastiche
of ancient epics,"[28] no longer excites the imagination. By and large
it remains either the preserve of the scholar interested in tracing the
origins of eighteenth-century thought or material for the specialist
devoted to exploring the development and meaning of French
rhetoric.

XIV   Evaluation

Despite its lack of appeal for the modern reader, *Télémaque* is, as
it once was, Fénelon's most famous book. One is therefore reluctant
to cast it aside with casual and flippant remarks. A masterpiece,
however, it is not; and few would be foolish enough to prefer it, as
did eighteenth-century critic Houdar de La Motte, to *The Iliad*. By
Fénelon's own admission it was "a story written hastily and in detached fragments" (7, 655), a factor which explains in part why it
may leave the reader with a feeling of monotony as well as a multitude of hurried impressions. As one modern critic, Alfred Adler,
puts it, "The careful reader would very much like to learn the lesson
of the entire book, but he feels that he has embarked on a
hasty flight from lesson to lesson, a flight from one tableau to
another. . . ."[29]

A more serious criticism, perhaps, is that, unlike Dante's *The
Divine Comedy*, for example, *Télémaque* possesses but little dramatic interest. On this point Saint Cyres, an early twentieth-century
critic, is particularly severe, but quite perceptive, I find, when he
states: "Fénelon, whose letters are a gallery of speaking portraits
equal to the pages of Saint Simon, could not endow the personages
of his story with life; Télémaque, Mentor, Philoctetes, Idomeneus,
flit by us cloudy and impalpable, the baseless fabric of a vision."[30]
An exception perhaps to this general view of Fénelon's characterization is found in his portrayal of Calypso. Here, I believe, the author
displays a decided flair for the dramatic; his beautiful and imperious
nymph exudes the grief, despair, and passion worthy of a well-
drawn tragic personage. She is Fénelon's incarnation of ancient tension and modern melancholy, his own configuration of human lust
and baneful love.

On the question of *Télémaque*'s style and language we come to
still another area where Fénelon has, at least from twentieth-century writers, not received the highest praise. The critic Arthur
Tilley, for example, feels that as a writer of poetic prose, Fénelon "is
some way behind the great masters of the art" (he refers specifically
to Bernardin de Saint-Pierre and Chateaubriand);[31] and Antoine
Adam professes greater interest in Fénelon's thought than in his
style which he condemns as possessing "too much softness" and "too
much indecision."[32] Jules Lemaître does not hesitate to characterize
the book's descriptions as "too general," too full of "ready-made
phrases."[33] Fénelon's language is indeed imprecise—even at times
quite banal—but it is rich in a harmony which to Goré is both
"precious and elegant."[34] It is this quality, as she explains, which at
least in part both irritates and discourages the modern reader.

Perhaps the time has come—or will soon come—for a reevalua-
tion of *Télémaque*. Whether or not it will ever become again a
revered classic is highly doubtful. "Nothing ages faster," says critic
Marc Soriano, "than a *livre de circonstance*" and what was exciting
and important for one generation suddenly becomes fragile and cold
for another.[35] The ideological and political content of *Télémaque* is
still capable, however, of attracting our attention. It is a work,
moreover, which should be carefully studied by those interested in
the development of children's literature; Fénelon may not be the
first to write for children, but he is surely one of the first to recognize that "the education of a prince, like any other child, is a political problem."[36] *Télémaque*'s tricentenary is yet some years away; it
is an occasion that may well provoke some stimulating discussion
and produce some needed exposure.

CHAPTER 6

The Political Reality

FÉNELON was born the year that Louis XIV attained his majority. By the time he had completed his theological training and made his entree in court circles, the Sun King's panoply of splendor and power had begun to reveal its chinks of social, moral, and political decay. In his efforts to establish a unified government and to centralize all authority for his purposes, Louis XIV had turned his kingdom into a despotic state where any sort of discontent was harshly repressed. His foreign policy, aimed at ensuring France's European preeminence by crushing the threats of Hapsburg domination, involved his country in a series of wars which, long before the struggle over Spanish succession, had brought France to the brink of financial ruin. The glitter, brilliance, and prosperity of the 1660s was by the late 1680s little more than a tarnished dream, scarcely capable of cloaking the poverty and economic distress of the nation.

The first reactions to Louis' abuse of royal authority came from Protestant writers and theologians who had left France in the wake of the religious persecution which followed the revocation of the Edict of Nantes. Among such figures was Pierre Jurieu (1637–1713), whose *Lettres pastorales* (*Pastoral Letters*, 1686–89), written from Holland, dared to attack the concept of a monarchial society. In the more than two decades following Jurieu's pronouncements—in fact, almost up to the time of Louis XIV's death—other voices within the kingdom, speaking the language of neither insurgency nor heresy, but daring to suggest reform within the system, were to be heard. Besides La Bruyère, who more as moralist than crusader underscored the defects of French society in *Les Caractères* (*Characters*), such men as Vauban (*Projet d'un dîme royale, Plan for a Royal Tax*, 1707) and Boisguillebert (*Détail de la France, Internal Economy of France*, 1695, 1707), proposed definite fiscal and economic reforms. To these names must be added that of Fénelon.

Fénelon's interest in political questions was not exactly a spontaneous one. Even before his appointment as preceptor, he had become closely allied with the Duc de Beauvillier and the Duc de Chevreuse, both of whom played a rather important role in Louis XIV's government. During the Saintonge mission he remained in contact with Seignelay, one of the king's ministers. It is not surprising, given these friendships and associations, to find certain indications of Fénelon's concern for political matters in the works written prior to 1689. Perhaps the most noteworthy example can be found in Chapter XI of the *Traité de l'éducation des filles*, where the following passage gives the reader a striking prevision of some of his later attitudes and opinions:

We know that their conquerors [the Greeks' and Romans'] did not scorn the idea of tilling the soil and returning to the plough after celebrating a victory. This is so far removed from our present customs that it would be impossible to believe such a thing were it not for the fact that historically we have no reason to doubt it. But is it not as natural for one to think of cultivating one's land as of defending it or extending it by force? What good is victory without the rewards of peace? After all, soundness of understanding consists of one's striving to be instructed correctly in the way those things fundamental to human existence are done; all the greatest issues depend on this. The strength and well-being of a nation consist not in possessing many poorly cultivated provinces, but in deriving from the lands it does possess everything it needs to feed a numerous population (5, 591).

Once he was associated with the Duc de Bourgogne, who, as he remained convinced, would one day rule France, Fénelon was prepared to make such a passing political observation as the one just cited an integral part of those fictional instructions which have already been discussed. Committed to a definite ideal, he was determined that his royal charge should become not only a wise and gracious ruler, but a Christian one as well.

Even in the face of disgrace and exile, Fénelon remained convinced that his role as mentor should continue. Despite his geographical separation from Versaille's sphere of influence, he managed to maintain a spiritual and ideological contact with the Beauvillier-Chevreuse coterie and with his former pupil. The age of fiction was over—of that he was well aware—but, whether through hope of future advancement and power or through his sheer refusal to remain silent, he saw the time had come for him to disclose and illuminate the more practical aspects of his political credo. This chapter proposes to discuss, using the *Lettre à Louis XIV* as a sort of prologue, Fénelon's major, nonfictional political works which reflect the stern realities of the years from 1697 to 1712.

I Lettre à Louis XIV

Long a standard anthology selection, the *Lettre à Louis XIV* was, however, unknown to most of the eighteenth century. When philosopher and mathematician D'Alembert delivered his eulogy of Fénelon before the Académie Française in 1774, he referred to the document, as he did again three years later at a special session of that group which was attended by Emperor Joseph of Austria.[1] Certain indications within the text—the allusion to the death of Louis XIV's war minister Louvois (1691) and the famine of 1693, as well as the diatribe against the Archbishop of Paris, Harlay, have led commentators to observe that the *Lettre* was written sometime between 1692 and 1695, most probably in either 1693 or 1694.[2] Published in 1785 in an edition of D'Alembert's *Histoire des membres de l'Académie Française* (*History of the Members of the French Academy*), the *Lettre à Louis XIV* remained subject to claims of inauthenticity until the discovery in 1825 by the publisher Renouard of a manuscript copy in Fénelon's own hand.

Bold, caustic, and direct, Fénelon's epistle to his sovereign was shielded by the mask of anonymity. It is scarcely conceivable that he expected Louis to be the direct recipient of such an attack; rather, it appears that he intended his message more for Madame de Maintenon and the Duc de Beauvillier (The "Mme de M. and M. le D. de B" referred to in the next-to-the-last paragraph), who, so he hoped, might counsel and advise the erring monarch.[3] Fénelon realized well that such weighty matters as he was inclined to discuss, such daring criticisms as he was willing to proffer would never reach Louis' ears by way of flattering and compliant courtiers.

After asking the king not to be astonished by his frankness, Fénelon sharply criticizes Louis' education and training for kingship. He blames those who were entrusted with instructing the king in the "science of governing" for his suspicious nature, his jealousy, his aversion to virtue, his "fear of all outstanding merit," and his predilection for "tractable and grovelling men" (7, 509). Equally guilty are the ministers of the government who have done nothing more than enforce arbitrary power. Although it may be true, Fénelon admits, that Louis has been "jealous of authority," basically "each minister has been the master within the domain of his ad-

ministration" (7, 510). Haughty, cruel, unjust, and violent, these
officials have in the final analysis been responsible for Louis' inure-
ment to flattery and for his odious reputation among neighboring
nations. Drawing their king into one armed conflict after another
over a period of twenty years, the ministers have succeeded in
either alienating or destroying all of France's former allies. The
Dutch war of 1672 is for Fénelon a case in point, a fine example of an
act of aggression which was but the beginning of all the havoc and
desolation produced by Louis in his quest for power and glory.
Instead of following the "pathway of truth and justice," instead of
adhering to the lessons of the Gospel which would have made him
the father of his subjects and the arbitrator for other nations, the
king has become "the common enemy" of his neighbors and "a hard
taskmaster" for his own people (7, 511).

Turning from questions of foreign policy, Fénelon next calls attention to the country's lamentable domestic condition, for which he
personally blames the king and his advisors. "All of France," he
declares, in lines now familiar to many a reader, "is nothing more
than one great desolate and unprovisioned poorhouse" (7, 511).
Hunger is rampant and the fields uncultivated; the artisans and
craftsmen are without work and the nobility ruined; commerce has
been all but destroyed. The people, "full of bitterness and despair,"
are now aware that their ruler is without pity and concern for their
plight. Seditious acts, Fénelon notes, are becoming more prevalent
throughout the kingdom; and the powers that be are now reduced
either to leaving civil disorder unpunished or to massacring the
citizens who can no longer bear starvation and taxation.

Louis XIV is, in Fénelon's estimation, a man who is living with "a
fatal blindfold tied about his eyes" (7, 511). His courage has been
replaced by his obsession for flattery, to the point that he now
avoids, out of fear that he might really learn the truth, those men
with the most solid judgment. Soon enough, warns Fénelon, God
will lift the veil which blurs his vision; His sword, which has been
slow to strike, will ultimately force this man, whose religion is
founded on fear, superstition, and formal practices, to conversion
through humiliation. For the moment, however, Louis, guided by a
scandalous and corrupt archbishop (Harlay, who was mentioned
earlier) and a confessor (Father La Chaise), who is likened to "the
blind leading the blind," remains insensitive to the evils within the
church and state. Woe unto such people as Beauvillier and Madame
de Maintenon, concludes Fénelon, if they do not speak truth to

their sovereign; if they do not urge him to seek humility, to restore peace to the land, to reject "the unjust counsel of political flatterers," and restore to his enemies those conquests which he cannot in any case retain without being unjust (7, 513).

Madame de Maintenon may well have taken Fénelon's words to heart, but her basic conclusion was that his message was too harsh and only likely to "irritate" and "discourage" the king.[4] The *Lettre à Louis XIV* is indeed a revealing example of his intense and bitter style.[5] Because this particular quality pervades the work, it is easy to forget that the letter is not completely negative in tone, and that Fénelon does in fact offer some definite constructive criticisms and proposals such as those which call for the alleviation of hunger and the reduction of taxes, and that he does support certain statements with concrete historical and political allusions. A careful reading of the text also illuminates its Christian aspect which emphasizes the necessity for truth and justice while espousing the idea of a benevolent, paternalistic, truly religious king devoted to the preservation of the integrity and the autonomy of the Church. Finally, the *Lettre*, written at the time Fénelon was beginning the composition of *Télémaque*, is a significant preamble to that later work in which many of the same principles will reappear, wrapped in the gentleness and charm of an adventure tale.

II   Examen de conscience sur les devoirs de la royauté

It is impossible to date with any certainty the work that stands as Fénelon's first real venture into the area of practical politics. The *Examen de conscience sur les devoirs de la royauté (Examination of Conscience on the Duties of Royalty)* as it has been generally known since its inclusion in the Versailles edition, may have been written as early as 1697, although speculation would have us believe it was composed around 1702, shortly after the Archbishop of Cambrai resumed his correspondence with his former pupil.[6] The latter, more than likely out of fear that the manuscript might fall into the hands of his grandfather, presumably handed it over to Beauvillier. At any rate, the *Examen* did not appear in print until 1734.[7]

The *Examen* is arranged as a series of three articles or sections (plus two supplementary discourses) containing in all thirty-eight questions, which are posed much in the manner of a priest preparing a faithful parishioner for confession. The decided religious character of the work is, in fact, underscored throughout a large part of the first article, entitled "Concerning the Instruction Necessary for a Prince." Without hesitation Fénelon asks the duke if he knows all the Christian truths, and if he is aware that it is under God's law that he must rule his people. This divine law is quite simply the Gospel, the great and guiding force for a king as well as for his subjects. It is in studying God's word and in praying for help in understanding the eternal truths, so Fénelon advises, that he will realize that political matters do not exempt him from being humble, just, sincere, and compassionate.

Having covered this matter of possible spiritual indifference and laxity, Fénelon next broaches a question that could well have come from the pages of the *Dialogues des morts, Télémaque*, and the *Lettre à Louis XIV*: "Have you not sought out advisors who are the most disposed to flatter your vanity, ambition, ostentation, weakness, and guile?" (7, 86). This query in turn leads to another which is nothing less than the archbishop's plea for his pupil to seek pious, steadfast, enlightened men to guide him; to employ the services of several advisors, so that one minister might shield him from the prejudice of the other. Everything considered, however, Fénelon regards these counselors as only consultants; for this reason a king should have a knowledge of the law and of the customs of his nation. He should know, moreover, the principles of jurisprudence and what he refers to as "the code." (Fénelon is referring to the Ordinance of 1697 or the Code Louis, as it was called.) As ruler he should be prepared to study "the true form" of his country's government, to take into account, for example, the limits of his authority through his awareness of the ancient parliaments, the Estates-General, and the evolution of internal affairs in general (7, 86–87). Finally, Fénelon counsels his prince to study the present so that he may be acquainted with statistics regarding population, in particular the demography relevant to the various professions and occupations of his subjects.

The second article presented under the rubric "Concerning the Example That a Prince Owes His Subjects," is in essence a miniature moral treatise wherein Fénelon elucidates certain principles that must guide the private life of a king. As head of the state, and therefore the most public of figures, he cannot expect to hide his evil. "Vice," the archbishop reminds his pupil, "is in itself a contagious poison," ready and waiting to be taken in by the human race (7, 87). What a ruler does and says immediately sets an example not only for his subjects, but for other nations and monarchs as well. In this section Fénelon specifically attacks the idea of having a large number of women at court, particularly those of dubious morality. In short, he envisions for his prince a sober milieu (not unlike that of Idomeneus' kingdom in *Télémaque*) devoid not only of the influence of "pernicious women" but also of "excessive lavishness" (7, 88). The luxurious living of the royal family will only serve to trigger a type of chain reaction whereby the prince will imitate the king, the gentleman will ape the lord, until finally the financier, in his effort to outshine the nobleman, will end up being emulated by the bourgeois. Fénelon therefore urges the duke to follow the great example that Louis IX set for "great simplicity" (7, 88). It is through moderation that a king can lead his subjects, not to speak of neighboring peoples, away from frivolity and back to the realm of good sense. Although Fénelon does not dare mention the name of Louis XIV, his ironic allusion to the "marvels of luxury into which we have fallen" and his direct reference to Burgundy clearly indicate, for example, that this section is far more than a veiled attack on the Sun King (7, 88).

The third article, "Concerning Justice Which Should Preside over All Governmental Acts," is the longest and probably the most important. Almost all the questions here are allusions that recall past attitudes and practices of Louis XIV.[8] The first "examinations" (7, 89–90) deal with the relation of the king to his people in matters of taxation ("Have you thoroughly considered the real needs of the state in order to compare them with the disadvantages of taxation before burdening your people?"), the appointment and conduct of ministers, administrators, and governors ("Have you made it clear that you are prepared to listen to grievances against them and to do justice in such cases?"), and his attitude toward the general welfare of the nation ("Have you consulted the most able and best-intentioned people who can instruct you about the condition of the provinces, farming, last year's harvests, the state of commerce, etc . . . ?"). Subsequent questions (7, 90–91) bring to light Fénelon's concern for such issues as the proliferation of appointed or created offices, which he describes as being only "disguised taxes"; the impressment of soldiers and sailors, denounced as cruel and inhuman; the mistreatment of galley slaves, who, as he reminds his prince, are often not paroled when their term expires; and the proper administration of the army, an organization which Fénelon depicts as poorly paid and badly disciplined.

As important and provocative as the preceding topics may be, no

single one occupies so great a focal position in the *Examen* as Fénelon's views on war and peace. These last two nouns must indeed be
considered a unit, for Fénelon, in his questions and statements to
the young prince, does not limit himself to denouncing the injustice
of territorial usurpation and the general idea of man's inhumanity to
man. His concern for a nation's conduct in the aftermath of hostilities prompts him to outline a series of principles, the very foundations of which are justice and humanity. Of particular interest
here is Fénelon's notion that peace treaties cannot be based on force
and trickery, a conviction which he had already expressed in his
Lettre à Louis XIV; they must be executed promptly and never
violated, as he says, "under fine pretexts" (7, 94). The idea of filling
a treaty "with ambiguous and captious terms" is a sure way of preparing for future wars (7, 92).

With the *Examen*, Fénelon has quite definitely cast aside his
vision of an ideal Salentum. While it may be true that he still har-
bors the illusion of a state that is guided by an active, strong, sincere, and well-informed ruler devoted to humanitarian principles,
Fénelon quite consciously reveals that he is haunted still, as it were,
by the specter of Louis XIV.[9] For this reason his dream of an enlightened monarchy is tinged with more than its fair share of reality,
with its sorrowful recognition of "the seeming inevitability of power
politics."[10] In the first supplement to the *Examen*, where he investigates the matter of defensive alliances and the balance of power,
Fénelon speaks of that day-to-day experience that teaches him that
"the greatest power always prevails" and that "each nation seeks to
triumph over the others around it" (7, 98). Such resignation, however, does not in the long run destroy the impressive quality of the
work. It would be difficult to find another seventeenth-century
writer who has treated with as much boldness and originality the
question of international relations, or one who has stated with as
much incisiveness (I am thinking particularly of the second supplement to the *Examen*) the conflicting ideas of Christian morality and
injurious despotism.[11]

III *The Letter to Louville (October 10, 1701)*

On February 18, 1701, the seventeen-year-old grandson of Louis
XIV, Philippe, Duc d'Anjou, entered Madrid to take up residence at
the Buen Retiro palace as Felipe V, the first of the Spanish Bour-

bons. Among those in his entourage, appointed as tutor and aide to the shy and awkward young king, was the Marquis de Louville, a man whose dubious historical fame rests principally on that appointment. In October of that same year, Fénelon addressed to the Marquis an advice-filled letter in which he also included what he considered necessary instructions for a young ruler.

For those who have read *Télémaque*, the *Dialogues des morts*, or the *Examen de conscience* (which more than likely dates approximately from the same period), Fénelon's ideas on kingship in this document have a more than familiar ring. He warns, for example, of flattery, "that trap to be feared by all good hearts," and he advises the young man "to obey the laws and not himself" (7, 548). He emphasizes, as he does particularly in *Télémaque* and the *Lettre à Louis XIV*, the need to encourage agriculture. He also requires the sovereign to set a good example for his subjects (a major precept of the *Examen*), to devote himself to the tranquility and happiness of his people, and to demonstrate his courage, not necessarily on the battlefield, but in the skillful management of the country's affairs. Generally speaking, Fénelon's conception of royal authority is founded on the principle of moderation and on the premise that "a king has no other honor nor interest than that of the nation which he governs" (7, 548).

The letter to Louville, although to a degree less practical than the *Examen*, has about it the quality of the latter work. It is marked not only by Fénelon's awareness of the moral and political problems facing any young monarch, but at the same time by his sincere encouragement: as a prince grows in experience, Fénelon is saying, so will his authority and acumen also increase. Written before the bitter French defeats of 1708 and 1709, this epistle is reflective of Fénelon's optimistic spirit, the very core of which will be challenged and tried to the extreme in the difficult years that follow.

IV   Discours pour le sacre de l'Electeur de Cologne
(Discourse for the Consecration of the Elector of Cologne)

In 1688, when he was only sixteen, Joseph Clement of Bavaria, without having taken even minor orders, became Elector and Archbishop of Cologne. During the War of the Spanish Succession, stripped of his kingdom by the Allies, he came as an exile to Lille, where he eventually fell under the influence of Fénelon who persuaded him to be consecrated. It was for this high and solemn occasion on May 1, 1707, that the discourse in question was composed. Although classed among Fénelon's sermons, the *Discours pour le sacre de l'Electeur de Cologne (Discourse for the Consecration of the Elector of Cologne)* has a very direct and significant political bearing, since it contains the author's "mature" estimation of the church and its relation to the state.[12]

The first point of this discourse, clearly announced in the exordium, is an exposition of the enduring, independent nature of the Church. By means of a panoramic, sweeping representation which recalls the technique and imagery of the Epiphany sermon, Fénelon strives to demonstrate that "despite the tempests from without and the scandals from within," the body of God's children has through the ages remained "immortal" (5, 606). Bound to the state, to which it owes obedience concerning temporal matters, the Church remains free, however, as far as spiritual functions are concerned. Rulers should remember, therefore, that by becoming the children of the Church, they have acquired in no way the right to subjugate the Church to their wishes, for it is an institution to be served, not dominated.

This does not mean, on the other hand, that the Church is in any way interested in political power: "It wishes only to obey; endlessly it sets the example of submission and zeal for legitimate authority; it would shed all its blood to uphold it . . . It seeks, not the riches of men, but their salvation . . . It accepts their perishable offerings only that it may give them eternal benefits" (5, 607).

Up to this point the tone of Fénelon's message has been firm but suave. In the closing paragraphs of the first section, however, he turns with almost eloquent vindictiveness to warn the kings of the earth of God's punishment if they attempt to persecute or humiliate Christ's bride. A temporal sovereign may well be "the bishop from without," but he has no rights and functions except for the following: he is to keep the Church free by protecting it against all enemies, and he is to support and uphold its decisions without interpreting them. Fénelon is so convinced of the Church's liberty that he seems almost willing to sacrifice its unity; even in the face of heresy and abuse, so he declares, "It has even more need of guarding its freedom" (5, 608). The Church accepts the protection of princes, but, "far from listening to worldly politics," it is careful to believe only the words of God's Son (5, 609).

The second point of the discourse has an obviously less crucial political relevance, since it outlines in some detail the spiritual duty and comportment of a prince (such as Joseph Clement) once he has become an active member of the clergy. This part of Fénelon's sermon is therefore a veritable *lettre de direction* for the elector, one which stresses the necessity for humility and urges the repression of pride and ostentation. It is, moreover, a fervent lesson in love, patience, and gentleness, virtues which can be attained through prayer and meditation. If a churchman of high and noble lineage, such as the one to whom this sermon is addressed, can exhibit such qualities, then his service to God's kingdom becomes all the more impressive and influential.

Fénelon's notion of an independent, autonomous Church may well seem at first glance to be a conceptual, almost fanciful product of his imagination. He was, however, always careful to shape his dreams and principles to divine will;[13] and his idealized view of the Church, which can be attributed principally to a metaphorical acceptance of that body as the "bride of Christ," is in reality more closely related to a variety of scriptural references (particularly Saint Paul) and the influence of Saint Augustine.[14] This is not to say, by any means, that Fénelon's ultramontane learnings are obscured: the *Discours pour le sacre de l'Electeur de Cologne* is a vigorous warning to any king—Louis XIV most certainly included—that the power and authority of the Pope are not to be usurped. Fénelon, unlike Bossuet, is far from proclaiming, "Kings . . . you are Gods."[15] He prefers instead to establish a political order, the key to which is not deference and gratitude, but mutual respect and Christian understanding. The problems involving the coexistence of Church and state will again occupy his mind some four years later, in the *Tables de Chaulnes*, where he will approach such issues with less emotion and more moderation.

V   *That Horrible Year of 1710*

No survey of Fénelon's political theories and attitudes would be complete without some consideration of his reaction to the effects of the War of the Spanish Succession. As stated earlier, he was no casual, timid observer safely hidden away in the drawing rooms of Versailles. His many letters and reports attest to his concern for France's involvement in a conflict which for him all but spelled disaster. Two documents from this period merit our special attention: the third of the *Mémoires concernant la Guerre de la Succes-*

sion d'Espagne (Memoirs Concerning the War of the Spanish Succession) and his rather well-known letter to the Duc de Chevreuse, both of which date from the year 1710.

A. *The* Mémoire sur la situation déplorable de la France en 1710
   (Memoir on the Deplorable Condition of France in 1710)

With no sign of peace in sight, Fénelon takes stock in this memorial of the lamentable conditions brought about by a costly, debilitating war. In words that recall the *Lettre à Louis XIV*, he speaks of France as "an old broken-down machine," ready to crack into pieces at the first shock (7, 159). One of his basic fears is that no one realizes the serious state of affairs. Not one of Louis XIV's ministers has been in a position to gather together all the diverse governmental issues and problems so that they might be studied as a totality. As a sort of necessary prelude to his corrective course of action, Fénelon catalogues for his reader (probably the Duc de Chevreuse) the various ills with which the French are plagued: the soldiers are not paid, and they are, moreover, poorly fed; the morale of the officers, who are scarcely better off, is low; the people, beset by pillaging and requisitions, fear the French army and the local officials as much as they do the enemy; the condition of the wounded is a wretched one, since there are no bandages and no medicine; farming in general has been disrupted. Added to this is Fénelon's general conclusion that France has sunk so low that she has become an object of public derision. He then adds: "There is no longer in our people, in our soldiers, and in our officers either affection, esteem, confidence that we will rise again, or fear of authority . . . Each person seeks only to dodge the rules and wait for the war to end at whatever price that may be" (7, 160).

The time has come for positive action, and the king must be prepared to make certain sacrifices. When peace negotiations, so badly handled up until now, are resumed, then France must act in good faith. She must be prepared to realize that if the abdication of the Spanish throne by Philippe will save her from peril and ruin, then this expediency must be accepted. It would be for the king, says Fénelon, "far less sad and shameful to dethrone him than to see him dethroned under his eyes by his enemies" (7, 163). Even in the face of a disadvantageous peace settlement, Louis XIV would have the opportunity of restoring the lost confidence of his neighbors; he would, moreover, be able to work for the rehabilitation of his king-

dom by effecting reforms in farming, commerce, and financial affairs. Certain conditions, however, Fénelon openly rejects. The
enemy, for example, are not to be allowed passage through France,
and they are to be granted no outposts (port cities like La Rochelle)
in French territory.

Fénelon's politics of peace emerge here as a lesson in the practical
and the objective; it may be, in fact, a lesson which is too practical.[16]
It is not so much that Fénelon is thinking of dishonorable peace; it is
more as if, with the voice of desperation, he is willing to accept the
end of hostilities at any price. Roland Mousnier, a modern scholar
who is anything but sympathetic to Fénelon's policies of war and
peace, finds, that they are patently unrealistic. He dismisses as
ridiculous, for example, Fénelon's idea that Louis XIV might allow
the Swiss, as neutrals, to guard such border towns as Douai, Cambrai, and Valenciennes. Mousnier concludes that Fénelon is like
those, who, "so frightened by the risk of being caught up by patriotic and party spirit, and so moved by the thought that they are not
rigorously just," end by adopting the enemy's point of view.[17]
Fénelon may be a "humanitarian pacifist," but I do not think it fair
to call him a "defeatist." Courage and valor, as he demonstrates in
Télémaque, have their place. Inept and ineffectual methods of war-
fare, on the other hand, can only lead to the destruction of a nation.

B.   *The Letter to Chevreuse (August 4, 1710)*

Composed probably some four or five months after the preceding
mémoire, the letter to Chevreuse bears further witness to Fénelon's
state of disillusionment. Although it clearly depicts the ravages of
war, placing before the reader the image of France as "a besieged
fortress" (7, 321), it is not, however, altogether repetitive of the
other document in question. For one thing, Fénelon is more openly
critical of Louis XIV. He concludes very quickly, in fact, that the
country's ills stem from the fact that the war, up to the present, has
been only "the king's affair" (7, 321). Louis' absolutism has produced
a schism that separates him from his subjects, and this state of affairs
cannot endure. The nation at large must somehow be apprised of
general governmental policies; it must be made to feel a part of the
war effort. This assessment leads Fénelon to his second point: he
suggests to Chevreuse that the king convoke an assembly of nota-
bles, to be comprised of men from various walks of life and from
different countries. It is to be hoped that through their counsels the

French might seek in some detail "the least stringent means of maintaining the common cause" (7, 321). The nation, in short, must save itself; but, first of all, the entire kingdom must be made to feel that "the wisest heads that can be found are working for the public good" (7, 322). In that way the reputation of a "scorned and hated government" can be rebuilt (7, 322).

Having laid this much groundwork, Fénelon proceeds to a direct discussion of financial affairs. He advocates, for example, that national funds be divided into three categories: an allotment derived from public revenue to be paid to the poorest citizens in full and to the rich only in part, a "reasonable" subsistence income for the court, and an allocation to be supplied by the nation at large for the military. No longer are the financiers and usurers to control France's fiscal operations; the king will henceforth be unable to pass money from "the hands of all the good families of the kingdom and from the people" into the hands of his creditors (7, 322).

For some readers this particular letter to Chevreuse, because of its attack on Louis XIV, might seem to be nothing more than a harsh and rasping sequel to the *Lettre à Louis XIV* and the *Examen de conscience*. It is well, however, to look beyond Fénelon's disenchanted vision of royal power gone awry and to note that here his specific ideas about tax reform and strict economic measures anticipate the program he will set forth in the *Tables de Chaulnes*. This letter is also significant in that it clearly shows (see division nine) that Fénelon—again, with some forethought of the talks at Chaulnes—has already begun to formulate in a rather cogent fashion the active role that the Duc de Bourgogne should play in national affairs. Finally, I do not believe it is possible to find in any of Fénelon's writing, except of course for *Télémaque* and the *Examen de conscience*, a more manifest denunciation of despotism, which, as he says, is "the cause of all our woes" (7, 323).

VI *The* Tables de Chaulnes *(The Chaulnes Tables)*

Slightly less than two months after the death of Louis "the Great Dauphin," Fénelon interrupted the train of his parochial and polemical occupations to express to the Duc de Chevreuse, in a letter of June 9, 1711, his desire to discuss with him at Chaulnes matters concerning spiritual and temporal authority. "I would limit myself," says Fénelon, "to making out a list, resembling a memorandum, which would record the result of each conversation"

(7, 343). The result of those meetings in November of that same year was a document, schematic, synoptic, but specific in nature, called *Plans de gouvernement concertés avec le Duc de Chevreuse pour être proposés au Duc de Bourgogne (Governmental Plans Preconcerted with the Duke of Chevreuse To Be Proposed to the Duke of Burgundy).* Better known as the *Tables de Chaulnes,* it was first published in part in Bausset's *Histoire de Fénelon* (1808 edition) and then included as a complete text in volume XXII of the Versailles edition. The *Tables* are presented under the heading of two "articles" or "plans," which are in turn subdivided into topical sections.

A. Article One *(The Present)*

Fénelon's first and most urgent statement concerns his desire for a rapid conclusion to the war, even if it means sacrificing Arras and Cambrai. He suggests that provisions and supplies be laid by in anticipation of the spring campaign. If the war effort must indeed be maintained, then the government should think of placing the army under the most able of generals, one who is trained in defensive tactics. There is no need for new field-marshals, but the appointment of a moderate number of lieutenant-generals is in order. This section also includes Fénelon's succinct evaluation of certain French generals (Villeroi, for example, is hard-working, orderly, and dignified; Harcourt, although possessing a good mind, has little experience) as well as a definite proposal for a war council or staff at court. This body is to be composed not only of field-marshals, but also of other men whose military expertise surpasses that of the secretary of state.

B. Article Two *(The Future)*

Assuming that the war is over and that peace has been achieved, Fénelon enlarges upon his criticisms of the military in the *Examen de conscience* by advocating here some definite reforms for the future: France is most certainly to avoid engaging in any sort of general European war. Her armed forces are to be reduced to 150,000 men and the number of fortified places, garrisons, and regiments is to be limited, mainly in the interest of economy. Talent, not tenure, is to be a major criterion for an officer's advancement. Fénelon's interest in the welfare of the enlisted man is evidenced by his suggestions that a soldier never be recruited by force, that he serve a definite period of five years, and that he receive good pay, food, and medical care. Disabled veterans are to be cared for, not at the central Hôtel des Invalides in Paris, but in their own respective villages and towns.

Fénelon's retrenchment of governmental spending is applied not only to military affairs but to the court at large. He asks first that all unnecessary pensions be eliminated. In succinct phrases that recall Mentor's more detailed recommendations for Salentum, he urges moderation in the disbursement of money for such items as furnishings, clothing, and carriages. The king's household is to operate under a strict economy, and such projects as the construction of new gardens are to be abandoned. The patronage of the arts is to be the concern of wealthy individuals. In general, Fénelon envisions the enactment of sumptuary laws which will hold in check royal finances and ensure a balanced budget.

It is more than obvious in the next section, "The Interior Administration of the Kingdom," that Fénelon favors a decentralized government. To that end, he recommends the establishment of an *assiette* (a small assembly or diet) that would function in each diocese. Composed of the bishop, the local noblemen, and the third estate, the body would have the power of levying taxes; it would, however, in turn be responsible to the individual provincial estate or *état particulier* whose membership would be made up of deputies from the small assembly. Finally, on the top rung of Fénelon's administrative ladder there is to be the Estates-General, comprising three deputies from each diocese: the bishop, one gentleman of high rank (elected by the nobles), and a representative of the third estate (to be chosen by members of his own class). This body, required to meet every three years, would have the authority to review the decisions of the other assemblies and to exercise its jurisdiction in areas such as justice, law and order, finances, war, alliances, and agriculture. As a necessary addendum to this legislative reform, Fénelon specifically calls for the abolition of certain taxes—the *gabelle* (the salt tax) and the *capitation* (the poll tax), for example— and an end, generally speaking, to France's arbitrary policies regarding taxation. Fénelon does not elaborate at great length, but it is clear that he opposes the system of tax farming. The levying of taxes is henceforth to be handled by the estates in each province.

The longest subdivision of article II, devoted to ecclesiastical matters, repeats much of the message found in the *Discours pour le sacre de l'Electeur de Cologne*. Defining first of all temporal power

("a co-active authority" responsible for ensuring man's just and virtuous social existence) and spiritual power ("a noncoactive authority" which teaches the faith, administers the sacraments, and over-
sees the practice of "evangelical virtues"), Fénelon continues by
reaffirming his belief in "the reciprocal independence" of church
and state (7, 184). He also reiterates his convictions concerning
mutual aid and cooperation, all of which leads to his drawing up a
rather long list of ways and means to preserve that desired relationship. The king, for example, may reject bulls that would tend to
usurp temporal authority, but he should reestablish free communication between the bishops and their leader. He should consult with
Rome about the procedure for deposing bishops, and he should
allow his most enlightened and pious subjects to elect popes. He is
to place in his council a few devout, learned, and moderate bishops
who might offer advice involving church and state (7, 186). Whereas
the king should work for either the reform or the suppression of
unedifying religious orders, he should, on the other hand, grant
bishops the freedom to visit, chastise, and dismiss priests and all
clergymen. Fénelon may have a basic fear of laic and gallican power,
but such reforms as these attest to his belief in a reciprocity of
responsibility and duty within a society founded on the principles of
justice and probity.

Fénelon's aristocratic tendencies are nowhere so visible as in the
Tables, where he proposes a whole series of reforms destined to
reconstitute and strengthen the nobility: a *nobiliaire* or peerage list
is to be carefully compiled in each province, and those families who
are not included in the central registry in Paris will not be recognized; the education of the nobility is to become the responsibility of
the king, who will choose a hundred children of the higher nobility
as pages, while appointing the sons of lesser families as regimental
cadets; positions in the king's household will be given only to those
of noble birth; the aristocracy will henceforth be allowed to enter
commerce and the magistracy with no fear of derogation. Fénelon
also specifies that no new titles of nobility be created except for
those who render conspicuous service to the state, and that royal
bastards no longer be given the rank of prince. Unlike Saint-Simon,
he does not dream of giving the aristocracy any sort of political
preponderancy; but he does wish to remodel the higher orders into
a vital and useful class, one which is both economically and socially
secure.[18]

The sixth subdivision presents Fénelon's plans for a reform of France's judiciary system. Basically, his view of justice is founded on the principle of simplification: few judges, few laws, and few tribunals. As in the case of military administration, he feels that merit, based on talent and performance, should be the guide in determining a magistrate's advancement. Nothing undermines the efficient administration of the law quite so much as the purchasing of offices and positions.

The remaining notes of the *Tables* concentrate on the subject of commerce. Although Fénelon stresses here, as in *Télémaque*, the need for "freedom," he condemns those who deal in luxury items. What is perhaps most prescient about his remarks is his attention to such matters as maritime laws, which should be designed to "neither vex nor rile foreigners," and his suggestion that France, without stifling or excluding competition, establish factories capable of producing better goods than other countries (7, 188).

C. *Conclusion*

Given its practical, reformatory nature, it may be tempting to judge the *Tables de Chaulnes* in either of two ways: we may tend to accept Fénelon's concrete vision as a configuration which is far less fascinating or remarkable than his idealized concepts;[19] or else, we may be inclined to dismiss Fénelon as some sort of hapless romantic, who, haunted by chimerical, pathetic notions, is reacting against Louis XIV's bourgeois absolutism.[20] There is indeed a strong reactionary, almost medieval, quality present in the *Tables*—seen particularly in Fénelon's approbation of an aristocratic élite and in his objection to laic power—but it is this characteristic, as Lemaître suggests, which accounts for the *Table's* powerful originality.[21] Unlike the Fénelon of utopian persuasion, here is a realist at work, a man who has not only a firm grasp of French history and a sound knowledge of its institutions, but one whose plans and aspirations are devised in the name of humanity and justice.

VII *The Epilogue: Some Precautionary Measures*

Fénelon's grief-stricken, despairing reaction to the Duc de Bourgogne's death is recorded in a letter of February 27, 1712, addressed to the Duc de Chevreuse: "I am gripped by horror, and without being sick, am suddenly chill. While mourning the prince whose death tears at my heart, I am alarmed for the living" (7, 374). The remainder of the message is in truth filled with his apprehension concerning the unconcluded peace, the advanced age of the king, and the thought that France might well have a regent. He urges Chevreuse to persuade Madame de Maintenon and the ministers to think of drawing up plans for a new government and of providing for the education of the young prince, the future Louis XV. Not long after the composition of this letter, Fénelon was approached by Beauviller who asked him to draft a governmental program. The response to this request was Fénelon's last political work, the four *Mémoires sur les précautions et les mesures à prendre après la mort du Duc de Bourgogne (Memoirs on the Precautions and Measures To Be Taken after the Death of the Duke of Burgundy)*, dated March 15, 1712.

The premature death of Fénelon's ex-pupil at age twenty-nine was clouded over by the rumor that he had been poisoned by the king's nephew, Philippe, Duc d'Orléans (1674–1723). The first *mémoire*, which discusses the pros and cons of an investigation of this alleged crime, voices Fénelon's basic doubts about the validity of such a procedure. Even if Orléans' guilt were proven—in itself a difficult task, given the fact that he is of such high rank—would it be possible, Fénelon asks, either to execute or imprison him? His first concern is for the safety of the king and young Prince Louis, and for this reason alone he recommends a highly secret inquiry into the matter. This *mémoire* may have only a limited historical and political interest, but it does reveal—in addition to Fénelon's unflattering portrait of Orléans and his daughter—the author's practical and cautious nature.

The second *mémoire* is in essence Fénelon's plea for certain internal reforms which he feels must be accomplished before France is beset by the problems of a regency. Still present in his thoughts are measures he has spoken of on more than one occasion: the quick negotiation of a peace settlement, the reordering of the country's finances, the fashioning of the army into a well-disciplined, reliable force, and the destruction of the Jansenist party. Paramount in his mind, however, is his plan for a council of regency. In the next report he explains in some detail his concept of this administrative body. Composed of both nobles and clergy, but excluding princes of the blood, the council would serve as a bulwark against the threats of anarchy and disorder. Without usurping the present king's authority, it would act as a type of transitional power which would accustom the country to a new form of government.

In the final *mémoire* Fénelon offers some suggestions concerning the education of the future Louis XV. Stressing the need for a firm and able governor, he goes so far as to nominate his old friend Beauvillier for this post. For preceptor he recommends no specific individual; he simply specifies that he should be an ecclesiastic, preferably a bishop. Seconded by a sub-governor and a sub-preceptor, the new tutor is to begin his pedagogical duties at once. Although the pupil has not reached "the ordinary age" (Louis XV was only two years old at this writing), it is possible for him to become acclimated to an instructional staff "who will imperceptibly begin his education" (7, 193).

Compared to the *Lettre à Louis XIV* and to the *Tables de Chaulnes*, Fénelon's last memorials are, to say the least, calm and undramatic statements. Dictated more by fear and desperation than anger and reproach, they reflect strongly the malaise and frustration of that end-of-reign era. They stand as proof, nonetheless, of his unfailing spirit of reform, the basis of which remains order and the well-being of his nation.

CHAPTER 7

The Apologist

FÉNELON was in many ways a born dialectician, but he lacked
the system of great philosophers as well as their creative spirit.
It is perhaps more fitting, then, to speak of those works discussed in
this chapter as "apologetic philosophy."[1] Having assimilated the
ideas of such thinkers as Plato, Cicero, Descartes, and Malebranche, Fénelon ended in the last decade of his life by transform-
ing the core of his metaphysical background into another kind of
didactic expression. In order to withstand the rising wave of free
thought and to combat any sort of unorthodox, heretical presence,
he produced a body of writing that stands as his monument to what
he considered the true, unfailing Christian life.

I   Traité de l'existence et des attributs de Dieu
(Treatise on the Existence and Attributes of God)

Fénelon's treatise on the existence of God is in reality two works
in one. The first part of the *Traité de l'existence et des attributs de
Dieu*, believed to be a product of the Cambrai years, was quite
possibly begun sometime around 1705,[2] but not published until
1712. Part II, more than likely a sketch that Fénelon undertook
during his tenure at Les Nouvelles Catholiques, may or may not be
the polished and expanded work he refers to in a letter to Chevreuse
in 1701. It did not appear, however, until 1718, when it was included in an edition of Fénelon's *Oeuvres philosophiques*. Little
read today, the *Traité de l'existence et des attributs de Dieu* was for
the early eighteenth century a rather popular and quite influential
work. In 1719 the *Mémoires de Trévoux* reported that the treatise
had been "translated in all the European languages."[3] Thomas Reid
(1710–1796), one of the figures of the "Scottish Enlightenment" who
may have read Fénelon's work in Boyer's English translation which
132

was published in 1713 (*A Demonstration of the Existence, Wisdom, and Omnipotence of God*), called the treatise's interpretation of Descartes "the most intelligible and the most favourable that I ever came across."[4] Although badly received, for example, by the disciples of Malebranche, the work seems to have had a particular effect on writers who were, more properly speaking, apologists and poets and who helped to reestablish a vogue for the proof of God's existence based on the marvels of the physical world.[5]

Fénelon's theodicy in Part I of the treatise, unlike that of Leibnitz, is not a justification of God, but rather a demonstration of His existence through the spectacle of nature's wonders. Casting aside for the moment "abstract truths" and "purely intellectual operations," Fénelon elects to develop the argument of final causes (1, 1). All of nature, he maintains, bears witness to "the infinite art of its author," and it is this art that is expressed in "an order, an arrangement, an industry, a purposeful design" (1, 2). Chance, having neither will nor intelligence, is incapable of preparing or arranging anything. Who could believe, Fénelon asks, that Homer's *Iliad* was composed by means of the random assembling of letters of the alphabet; or that the colors of a painting, splashed and mingled upon the canvas, had by some chance arranged themselves to form a work of beauty and genius? Every beautiful work, in short, is born of a superior will; no sensible man can then deny that universal order bespeaks the presence of a providential force.

Having shown the relationship of order to works of the intelligence, Fénelon seeks to demonstrate how nature has an intelligent cause. To prove the existence of order in the physical universe he proceeds from more elementary considerations to those that are more complex. The first of these is what he calls "the general structure of the universe," a source of wonder for the reflective person who (unlike the awed and frightened Pascal) contemplates with curiosity "the almost infinite abysses by which he is surrounded on all sides" (1, 4). His admiration becomes evident when he realizes his position with regard to "the mass of the universe" (1, 4). Next to be taken into account are the basic elements—earth, water, air, and fire—all of which reveal an amazing providential design or a planned economy. Fénelon's view of nature is once more Virgilian, a serene and classic force united to man in order to nourish and support him. Even the ocean, for example, which at first glance seems destined to separate man, is "on the contrary the rendezvous of all peoples who would be unable to go by land from one end of the earth to the other" (1, 6).

This idea of harmony can also be applied to the animal world where each species "shows how much the craftsmanship of the worker surpasses the base material which he has fashioned" (1, 11). Fénelon may refer to "the machine of the animal," but without questioning the intelligence of the lower forms he underscores his admiration (using this word once more) for the process that created them by pointing out their instinct for preservation, their ability to renew their strength, and their power to reproduce. This exploration of order brings him finally to the pinnacle of his ascendant scale, that is, to man himself. Man's bodily proportions and functions may be still another source of admiration, but it is the mind, provided with faculties of sense perception and memory, that lifts him to the level of ideas and reason. It is the mind, though limited and weak, that is capable of conceiving and understanding the infinite. This, for Fénelon, is the decisive proof of the existence of God.

By rejecting any sort of rational approach, Fénelon makes of Part I a treatise that is consciously immune to the mathematical and scientific structure of the physical world. Seemingly indifferent to the theories of either Ptolemy or Copernicus, he speaks first of the earth as a globe "which is immobile" (1, 4) and then later as a body which turns "so regularly" about the sun (1, 8). He has adopted, in his own words, "a sensible and popular philosophy" (1, 2) whose apologetic method, commonplace by the sixteenth century, is rooted in the ancient world—in Cicero (most particularly the *De Natura Deorum*) and in Saint Gregory Nazianzen. Except perhaps for the final pages where he relies to some extent on metaphysical concepts and subtle analyses, this part of the treatise finds its strength in a poetic force which exhalts the beauty of creation as reflected in the creator. With a providential finalism that is so apparent in the harmonious nature of one of his eighteenth-century admirers, Bernardin de Saint-Pierre, Fénelon sings his own uncomplicated and unsophisticated hymn to the cosmos.[6]

The second part of the treatise represents an entirely different approach to Fénelon's philosophical problem, for here he appropriates a method that is basically Cartesian and that though neither popular nor scientific, is intellectual. At the very beginning he states his need for "the complete certainty of things" (1, 45). He can no longer accept either sense impressions or principles, since they represent only probability. Recognizing the power of illusion, he is like a man who is caught between philosophic doubt, "which alone is reasonable," and "the deceptive dream of everyday life" (1, 46). In order to defend himself against this continual deception, he must make use of the "clear idea" (l'idée claire"), that very principle of certitude, that "light within him," carrying him along and forcing him to judge and examine (1, 47). This process of consultation, his "universal key to all truth," becomes then the springboard to his system, whereby doubt gives way to thought, and thought to certainty (1, 53).

Fénelon's doubt is, like Descartes', methodical. It leads him to demonstrate God's existence by a series of proofs, the first of which is based on the imperfection of the human being. Man's errors, his ignorance, his uncertainty point toward one unassailable conclusion: that his being does not exist by itself and that there is the truth of an outside force, a necessary being who is "infinitely perfect" and who is ("la vérité d'autrui") called God (1, 54). This concept leads to the second proof, drawn from the clear and positive idea that we have of the infinite. Whereas the word *finite* is synonymous with that which is negative, the term *infinite* is affirmative; it denies the possibility of limits and thereby establishes a place for the precise and the positive. The idea of the infinite is not born of nothingness, nor is it invented. Having come from the outside, it exists within the individual as a part of that individual. "I cannot," says Fénelon, "erase it, nor can I either obscure, lessen, or contradict it . . . It does not depend on me; it is I who depend on it" (1, 56). If a person perceives the infinite present in his mind, he must then conclude that the true representation of the infinite must have something infinite in order to resemble and to represent it. Equipped with the idea of the infinite and infinite perfection, Fénelon next introduces his third proof: the idea of the necessary being. Since man is capable of recognizing that he himself is not this being, he must accept the certainty that he has received his existence through a single necessary being who created all others. Just as one can affirm his existence through thought, so must one accept the concept of existence based on the idea of an infinitely perfect being.

From these proofs Fénelon infers the existence of God, not only as an infinite and perfect being, but one who subsists by Himself ("par lui-même"). Nothing else need be added, for He is simple and indivisible. This absolute or perfect unity, this totality of being, means that He must possess "in virtue and in degree of perfection what He cannot have in quantity and scope" (1, 65). Rather than "extensive," God's degrees of perfection are "intensive." Since the perception of these degrees is what we call "the consultation of our ideas," it is easy to see how our ideas are imperfect (1, 65). God does not show us all the infinite degrees of being that are within Him; He limits us, says Fénelon, to those that we need for the purposes of understanding in this life.

In the last chapter of his treatise Fénelon strives to reveal the nature and attributes of God. After depicting Him as "all there is that is real and positive in minds, all there is that is real and positive in bodies," he concludes that "He is no more spirit than body" (1, 69–70). If He were only a spirit, He would have no power over corporal nature, nor would He have any relationship to what is contained in bodily form. At that point He would be unable "either to produce it, conserve it, or set it in motion" (1, 70). Another of Fénelon's major concerns in the final pages is to reconcile God's absolute simplicity with the multiplicity of divine attributes. Man may conceive of his creator as a multifaceted being, but he must remember that His infinite intelligence, power, goodness, and will "are one and the same thing" (1, 76).

Fénelon's metaphysical voyage in Part II, begun under the guidance of Descartes, is one that, in the final analysis, follows a more subtle, more poetic route. Distinctly less forceful than the author of the *Discours de la méthode*, Fénelon, despite his use of methodic doubt, abandons a cold and rational inquiry to seek a region where the intellectual and the mystical are capable of fusing. He chooses to make God present to the reason, but his "clear ideas" become modes of thought that take on an Augustinian, Platonic sense as he tries to elucidate the meaning of a unified, supreme being.[7] At the same time, Fénelon owes much to Malebranche: although he does not accept the latter's idea of a perfect world, he does, on the other hand, affirm the continuity and eternity of divine action and the concept of an infinitely perfect being.[8] Also, despite his apparent hostility towards Spinoza (in Chapter III of Part II, without actually naming that philosopher, he composes a "Réfutation de Spinoza"), Fénelon seems to embrace the Dutch philosopher's belief in totality of all being or unity of substance. His belief in God's immensity and omnipresence also leads him quite close to the borders of Spinozan pantheism. What originality Fénelon achieves in his treatise is probably due to his adaptation of Descartes, Malebranche, and Spinoza to the demands of his mystical, Guyonian tendencies.[9] As he states in his unfinished *La Nature de l'homme*, "I conceive in all of nature only two sorts of beings, the being who exists by itself and the beings who exist only through that first being."[10] It is this same principle—God as everything and the creature as nothing—that pervades his treatise and makes it for the most part a work that is as emotional as it is rational.

II   Lettres sur l'autorité de l'Eglise *(Letters on the Authority of the Church)*

Fénelon's return to the subject of Catholic authority is represented by the eight letters that he wrote probably around 1708[11] to two Protestants who were in the process of being converted. As the *Histoire littéraire de Fénelon (Literary History of Fénelon)* suggests, the first five, taken as a unit, offer a more complete doctrinal approach to the question than the other three (1, 19). Although Letters I, II, III, and IV strongly expound the idea of "one single, true religion" (1, 202), their rather brief, compact messages are bound together thematically by the stress that Fénelon puts on the necessity for humility and the defeat of one's pride. "A man," says Fénelon in Letter I, "can reason with another man, but with God he can only pray, be humble, remain silent, and blindly follow" (1, 202). Even the most enlightened people, he writes in Letter II, "need to humble their minds to a visible authority" (1, 202). Religion, in fact, is only humility, and one must believe without understanding. It is, of course, as Fénelon concludes in Letter IV, the Catholic religion that can give the necessary lessons in humility. Protestantism, he declares, encourages "natural presumption," whereas the convert's newfound faith will teach him to seek the kingdom of God within himself and to silence himself so that he might "listen to the spirit of grace" (1, 204).

Letter V, more expansive than the preceding four, is composed of a series of what Fénelon calls principal "reflections" necessary for the new convert. The first and third of these repeat a basic exhortation of Letter III, the necessity of "listening to the Church" (1, 204). This Church does not refer to several churches, but to the one that has remained "unique, universal, and subsistent throughout all the centuries" (1, 204). Using the same metaphor found in the *Sermon pour la fête de l'Epiphanie* (5, 620), Fénelon reminds his Protestant correspondent that the Church "is the city built on the summit of the mountain which all people see from afar; each person knows the place where he can find it, see it, and consult it" (1, 204). Whoever refuses to listen to it or believe it must be cut away from the society of God's children, as if he or she were "a pagan or a publican" (1, 205). The fourth reflection reiterates an important point of Letter III: the advisability of reform from within instead of outside the Church. Patience, caution, and zeal are required to keep unity and to work for what Fénelon terms "peaceful reform" (1, 205). Meanwhile, the new convert, as he is informed in the remaining instructions, is to acknowledge the reality of Catholic solidarity. To do so he must renounce his parents and friends and join the other self-sacrificing, simple believers "who live by faith and prayer" (1, 206).

Even though it is probable that Letters VI, VII, and VIII were addressed to an individual other than the one for whom the first five were intended, they add little to Fénelon's doctrine of infallibility, unity, and pure faith. Letter VII does, however, contain an interesting section wherein the Protestant gentleman in question is forewarned against the danger of accepting his own views as "supernatural lights" and his own desires as "God's will" (1, 213). It seems evident that Fénelon is reacting against the Illuminism of certain Protestant sects when he cautions that everything that is experienced within oneself is not necessarily passive, nor does it bear God's imprint. This "interior direction," based on immediate inspiration, is a type of fanaticism which rejects the counterbalancing forces of authority and "exterior law" (1, 213).

The *Lettres sur l'autorité de l'Eglise* (*Letters on the Authority of the Church*) repeat much of the basic substance of the *Traité du ministère des pasteurs* (*Treatise on the Ministry of Pastors*) and the *Sermon pour la profession religieuse d'une nouvelle convertie* (*Sermon for the Act of Profession of a New Convert*). Like those works, they are also indicative of Fénelon's simple, direct, and practical approach to matters of theological explanation, particularly when his instruction involves the untrained, unspecialized mind. Perhaps the greatest attraction of these letters is their intimate, personal nature, a quality that is inherent in Fénelon's persuasive and charismatic personality. This does not mean that he speaks the language of compromise; so far as he is concerned, the way to true faith is cloaked in dark shadows and personal sacrifice.

III   Lettres sur divers sujets de métaphysique et de religion

Presented in the Paris edition as a collection of seven letters, five of which bear the date 1713, the *Lettres sur divers sujects de métaphysique et de religion (Letters on Various Metaphysical and Religious Subjects)* represent still another phase of Fénelon's apologetic endeavor. Except possibly for one (V), addressed, as Gosselin claims (1, 9), to a Protestant, these epistles are intended for the Catholic freethinker, the individual whose philosophical and theological ruminations have resulted in his refusal either to accept the dogma and ritual of the Church or to obey its moral law. The first edition of the *Lettres sur divers sujets de métaphysique et de religion*, containing only Letters I, II, IV, V, and VII, appeared in 1718. They were reprinted in 1731 and again in Father Querbeuf's 1791 edition, which, incidentally, included the missing third and sixth letters (1, 11).

Letters I, II, and III have a particular interest since we know they were written specifically for the future regent, the Duc d'Orléans. Educated in part by the Abbé Dubois, whom modern historians Will and Ariel Durant refer to as an "ecclesiastical rake,"[12] Philippe was well known by this time for his idleness, debauchery, and his public affectation of impiety. He had, however, turned to Fénelon, perhaps more as thinker and philosopher than priest, for his views regarding certain theological matters. In compliance with this request, the duke received during 1713 a series of three letters.

The first of these, entitled "On the Existence of God and on Religion," is a sort of natural corollary to the treatise discussed above. In three divisions designated as chapters, Fénelon discusses first the origin and creation of man's thought, "that high degree of being," portraying it as a quality of freedom that was passed along to us through the beneficence of a superior being who possesses infinite perfection (1, 91). Chapter II is an echo of Part I of the *Traité de l'existence de Dieu*, an abbreviated attestation of God's existence as witnessed by man's physical endowments and the wonders of nature; while Chapter III argues the existence of a creative force, one which is superior to man's, since it was capable of fashioning, arranging, and conducting the universe with art and order and infusing blind, insensitive matter with thought. The remaining three divisions deal with man's worship of God, a necessary, outward, and public manner of expressing our love for and debt to our Creator and of awakening "in each other the memory of this worship which is within" (1, 97). Fénelon reminds the duke that through the ages there have been true worshipers of God, but of all the ancient peoples, only the Jews demonstrated a true and worthy religion— the adoration of one true God based on the fundamental principle of love. It was, however, Christ who joined together all the characteristics of the Jewish Messiah; and who brought to us a "cult for love," consisting not of burnt offerings and sacrificial animals, but one based on "renouncing ourselves so as not to love ourselves more than Him" (1, 100).

The second letter further considers the question of worship, delving with more incisiveness and thoroughness into the matter of its internal and external varieties. Here Fénelon emphasizes more strongly than in Letter I the suppression of the ego, the *moi* as he refers to it, so that man might use his intelligence to know God and his will to love Him. It is, indeed, this reign of God within us that constitutes true interior worship but it does not obviate in any way exterior ceremonies which help men "recall and remember God's graces" (1, 103). With special care Fénelon depicts the superior being as one who is "wise, good, vigilant," who wants to be known, loved, and obeyed (1, 105). Fénelon cannot understand how man, "so credulous with regard to everything that flatters his pride and his passions," can have any fear about either the scriptual promise concerning the immortality of the soul or the presence of free will (1, 116).

Although Letter III is really no more than a development of the first two, it does enforce with power and clarity the need for man to subordinate his interests to the Almighty's will. This type of conformity is synonymous with interior worship, which, expressed another way, is the individual's relation to God through thought and will. While reaffirming human liberty, Fénelon at the same time informs his correspondent that free will does not signify independence. All of God's creation is in His hands, and it is well to remember that man, that "vile nothingness called into being through His pure goodness," must love the Creator above all (1, 120).

Letter IV is of interest in that it shows us a Fénelon who openly declares himself "docile to the authority of religion" and "indocile to all philosophic authority" (1, 124). It is philosophy that he equates with reason, and he more than clearly prefers God's reason to his own. That is at least the major basis for his uncompromising rejection of Descartes, "who dared shake off the yoke of all authority to follow only his own ideas" (1, 124). In matters of pure philosophy he would much prefer to read Saint Augustine, who was able to conciliate his thought with religion. Fénelon also speaks of his dislike for Descartes' "indefinite world" and calls his theory of the void "a pure paralogism, wherein he followed his imagination rather than following purely intellectual ideas" (1, 124). This letter concludes with Fénelon's explanation of infinity, which, as elsewhere, he visualizes as "one, true, and perfect" (1, 126), and with his proof (also contained in the *Réfutation du système du Père Malebranche*) that God possesses a freedom and arbitrary power with regard to creation.

In the next letter (V), which may have been written to a Protestant (1,9), Fénelon adds but slight variation to his now-familiar themes of self-renouncement, Christian love, and humility. He accentuates, as in the *Lettres sur l'autorité de l'Eglise*, a need for a supreme authority—the Catholic church—which is capable of holding in check man's presumption and prejudice and filling him with needed certainty about spiritual matters. As in the case of Letter IV, he directs his correspondent away from the study of Descartes and more toward an appreciation of Saint Augustine. Once more he indulges in a refutation of Spinoza, this time referring to that philosopher by name and calling his followers "a sect of liars" (1, 129). What Fénelon cannot accept is the possibility of a divisible infinity; but again he illustrates that either he has read Spinoza too rapidly (and thereby misconstrued his ideas) or that he is too anxious to discredit a philosopher who was considered dangerous. Contrary to his attitude toward Malebranche, Fénelon is unwilling to examine him with any sympathy. He regards Spinoza's theses, to use scholar Paul Vernière's words, as "only a system of references or rather a seies of dangerous limits, a type of intellectual Inferno, the boundaries of which were not to be approached."[13]

Letter VI, which begins as a chatty message about the poor state of his health and his recently completed portrait (no doubt the one by Vivien), quickly moves to more serious matters as Fénelon urges the individual to free himself from pride and philosophic doubt. What he has in mind is actually a transformation, a gradual spiritual voyage of sorts whereby the soul, aided by grace and Providence, passes from reason to faith. Fénelon believes that the most sublime wisdom of the Word is already in man; it must gradually unfold so that it may be distinguished from reason. Once man is prepared to break the ego and to allow those "interior dispositions" (1, 138) to act, he will be able to realize that the Christian religion is "only the love of God," and that "the love of God is precisely this religion" (1, 140).

The last of the letters (and the shortest) is still another effort to lead the erring soul from the "blind, unbridled, insatiable, tyrannical" demands of self-love and from the "monstrous ingratitude" of his refusal to acknowledge, fear, and love God (1, 143). This composition is basically more instructional than the others since it traces in plain, specific language a plan for the Christian life. After advocating in general terms the individual's need to renounce pleasure and sensuality, Fénelon advises him to seek the company of those who believe and act as he does, to regulate his spending, to fill his leisure hours with useful occupations (such as the reading of books of piety), and to reserve a small amount of time both in the morning and the evening for prayer. Above all, the Christian is to listen to God; he is to remember, in the words of Jesus, that "the kingdom of God is within you" (1, 146).

The *Lettres sur divers sujets de métaphysique et de religion*, in much the same way as the *Traité de l'existence de Dieu*, can make but few claims to achievement in the realm of metaphysics or philosophy. Rather than seeking a definite system of proofs or indulging in speculation which might appeal to the questioning mind, Fénelon relies more on the heart than he does on reason. What binds this particular group of letters together is the author's insistence on the superior enlightenment of faith—not philosophical wisdom or pretence—and the invincible power of Christian love. Fénelon, as elsewhere in his spiritual writings, succeeds in combining thought with feeling and the sublimity of declamation with clarity and precision.

IV *Fénelon and the Jansenist Controversy*

Until his arrival in Cambrai, Fénelon, like others of his generation, had paid little attention to Jansenism. For some ten years following the "Peace of the Church," effected by Pope Clement IX in 1669, that austere wing of Catholicism had managed to attract little attention and to avoid the hostility of both temporal and ecclesiastical authority. In spite of the spasmodic persecution that followed the death of their great protectress, the Duchesse de Longueville, in 1679, the Jansenists continued in a silent and forceful manner to strengthen their position and win sympathizers. In Fénelon's diocese, where the influence of the Jansenists had been particularly strong for many years, they gave every indication of threatening the monopoly of the Jesuits as educators and moralists. It is small wonder, then, that Fénelon quickly became aware of their latent strength.

When the controversy over the *Cas de conscience* and the question of "respectful silence" erupted, Fénelon's state of consciousness concerning the ramifications of the Jansenist creed was awakened. Even then he was reticent to become involved in the dispute, aware that he could easily be accused of seeking to avenge himself on a faction that had in part been responsible for his disgrace. Whether or not he was in fact politically motivated, we shall never really know; but the fact remains that after the Pope's condemnation of the *Cas de conscience* in February, 1703, Fénelon gradually became convinced that this decision should be defended.

Among his first writings on the subject of Jansenism were four very long pastoral instructions intended as a justification and explanation of the infallibility of the Church. The first of these, dated February 10, 1704, establishes this doctrine on the basis of (1) the very words of the Scripture, that is, on promises made to the Church; (2) the continuous practice of the Church in regulating the faith of its members through the condemnation or approval of certain texts; (3) the authority of the French clergy, who, from the beginning, recognized this infallibility; (4) the inconsistency of the Jansenists who, on one hand, accept the Church's authority in approving the writings of Saint Augustine, but then reject it when the doctrine of Jansenius is condemned; and (5) the past actions of ecclesiastical councils which did not hesitate to judge the orthodoxy of books submitted for their examination. In subsequent instructions, written from early March to late April of 1705, Fénelon continued to develop his ideas. The *Seconde Instruction* (March 2, 1705) is significant, since it introduces, for example, the concept of a "supernatural" infallibility, whereby the Church is placed through Christ's promise "above the subtle arguments and endless discussions of the critics" (4, 69).

Fénelon's defense of infallibility was convincing and influential,

but it was unquestionably the pressure from Louis XIV and the
French Jesuits that induced Pope Clement XI to issue in July, 1705,
the bull *Vineam Domine Sabaoth,* condemning those who had
signed Alexander VII's original formulary with mental reservations
and confirming Rome's previous decrees concerning Jansenius'
work. Although Clement's decision really needed no clarification,
Fénelon responded with an *Ordonnance et instruction pastorale*
(March 1, 1706), a work designed to explain in simple terms to the
clergy and people of his diocese the implications of the Pope's con-
stitution. He also wrote during this period a series of letters to the
Bishop of Meaux (Monsieur Bissy) and to the Bishop of Saint-Pons,
who had remained sympathetic to the Jansenist cause.

The 1705 bull had presumably brought to an end the discussions
concerning respectful silence and infallibility. Soon, however,
another quarrel ensued, this time centered about the doctrine of
Father Pasquier Quesnel. This Oratorian, considered since the
death of Arnauld (1693) and Nicole (1695) to be the leader of the
Jansenists, was the author of the *Réflexions morales sur le Nouveau
Testament (Moral Reflections on the New Testament,* 1671). A very
successful work, it had been regarded for some years as a pious,
orthodox book; after 1696, however, the extreme Jansenistic tenets
of the *Réflexions* (for example, the power of grace, the futility of
human works, the need for every Christian to have access to the
Scripture) began to come under close scrutiny. Most of all, the
doctrine of Quesnel gave the Jesuits a basis for waging a direct
campaign against Cardinal de Noailles, who had remained sympathetic to the Jansenist cause.

Fénelon's relations with Quesnel began in a polite, charitable
manner. By 1710, however, after reading certain Jansenist publica-
tions (concerning Clement XI and the 1705 bull) which he regarded
as libelous and blasphemous, Fénelon openly laid at his feet the
responsibility for such revolting and scandalous statements. He felt
that it was up to Quesnel as leader of his party "to answer for their
writings and to rectify them when need be" (4, 582). Quesnel responded in 1711 with two invective-filled letters which Fénelon
never answered. Later that same year Louis XIV revoked the royal
privilege of the *Réflexions* and asked the Pope for a bull condemning
it. Rome's support came once more, in September, 1713, when the
now-famous bull *Unigenitus* was issued. The new promulgation did
not, however, end the debate, for the French clergy, many of whom

considered it a political battle of Gallican versus Ultramontane, were divided on the question. Fénelon labored hard for the acceptance of the *Unigenitus*, but, like Louis XIV, he would not live to see its full acceptance since the Parliament of Paris did not register the bull until 1720.

In the midst of the Quesnel controversy, Fénelon set about composing what was to be one of his last and best-known writings on the subject of Jansenism. Published in 1714, the *Instruction pastorale en forme de dialogues sur le système de Jansenius (Pastoral Instruction in the Form of Dialogues on the System of Jansenius)* was designed as a work, so he informed the Duc de Chevreuse in 1712, "to be read and understood by the majority of people" (7, 379). By dint of another statement in that same letter, it is obvious that he was influenced to some degree by the vivacity and spirit of Pascal's *Lettres provinciales (Provincial Letters,* 1656–57). Fénelon's novelty of treatment lies, of course, in the fact that he took a theological subject that was more or less thorny and uninteresting for the lay mind and encapsulated it in a semidramatic and popular form which he had previously used with success.

The work is divided into three parts containing in all, besides an introduction, twenty-four letters in which the author reports his discussion with two fictional characters, M. Fremont, a Jansenist, and M. Perrault, who is portrayed as having been convinced of the errors of Jansenism six months earlier. After justifying the form of this *instruction* and denouncing in general terms the Jansenist system (" . . . more shameful than that of the Epicureans," 5, 226), Fénelon attempts to show in Part I that it is "a very real heresy" (5, 229), consistent with the necessitous grace of Calvinism in its adherence to efficacious grace (impossible for the sinner either to hope for or merit through works); and that the Jansenists have abused the authority of Saint Augustine, whom they have erroneously interpreted. In Part II the author discusses for his interlocutor some of Augustine's principal works (the *De Gratia Christi* and the *De Libero Arbitrio,* for example) in order to show just how divergent the two doctrines actually are. He also proposes to M. Fremont that Jansenist doctrine stands opposed to that of Saint Thomas. Part III reveals Fénelon's views of Jansenism as a new doctrine, contrary to Christian spirit and dangerous for the true believer's morals. The colloquy ends, as one might expect, with the confusion of M. Fremont, whose arguments cannot match those of the author.

Fénelon's anti-Jansenist dialogues possess a certain dramatic thrust; they are as entertaining and lucid as the subject permits, but, having lost, like all his works in this theological area, most of their actuality, they are of little interest except to the very specialized. What possibly could fascinate us more than anything else is to remember that Fénelon, of all the great Christian figures of his time, was really the only one who was able to resist completely the Jansenist temptation.[14] Unable to deny man his freedom of will under any circumstances, he prefers to see this liberty as a weakness. It is, however, a weakness that can be overcome with the help of God who intervenes to make up for our shortcomings, and who, in the final analysis, strengthens our will and enlightens our thoughts.[15]

CHAPTER 8

The Lettre à l'Académie

ON November 23, 1713, by formal declaration, the Académie Française decided that each of its members was to submit opinions concerning new projects to be undertaken by that body. Since the ideas contained in the Abbé de Saint-Pierre's *Discours sur les travaux de l'Académie Française (Discourse on the Occupations of the French Academy,* 1712) had stirred up a fairly heated debate, the academicians were particularly anxious to have a variety of other reactions. Although for all intents and purposes an exile, Fénelon was by no means excluded from the survey. Interested particularly in the Quarrel of the Ancients and Moderns, and recognizing that this would be an excellent occasion to stretch his polemical muscles, as it were, he drafted a reply which reached the Academy in the spring of 1714. This version of the *Lettre à l'Académie (Letter to the Academy),* read before the membership on May 26 (it has not survived), so impressed his colleagues that they secured Fénelon's permission to print the document. He in turn asked permission to revise his critical statement, which by the time it reached the Academy in October of 1714 obviously exceeded the limits set by the demands of a routine academic memorandum. This work, known first as the *Réflexions sur la grammaire, la rhétorique, la poétique et l'histoire (Reflections on the Grammar, the Rhetoric, the Poetics, and the Treatise on History),* was published in 1716 more than a year after the death of Fénelon.

I *The Dictionary and the Grammar*

Of all the projects sanctioned by the original statutes of the Académie Française in 1634, the preparation of a dictionary was the only one that had been realized by the time Fénelon wrote his *Lettre.* In 1694, after more than half a century of delays and difficulties, a two-volume *Dictionnaire de l'Académie Française (The*

Academy Dictionary) was published in Paris. Intended as a compendium of words that were acceptable from a literary standpoint (technical terms were excluded), this work was comprised of entries grouped according to families or roots. The second edition of the *Dictionnaire*, with an alphabetical arrangement, would not appear until 1718.

Fénelon chose to begin his recommendations to the Academy on the subject of this still incomplete work. After praising the undertaking, he reminds his readers that usage, the great controlling factor of language, will gradually render the new dictionary—at least to a large degree—obsolete. Given this eventuality, what Fénelon chooses to stress first is its particular use for foreigners who might wish to read the masterpieces of French literature. Next to be considered is the possibility that such a work will also serve as a useful guide for certain cultivated Frenchmen ("les plus polis"), who on occasion may be in doubt regarding the precise meaning of a word. Finally, Fénelon points out how valuable it will be in aiding future generations to understand "the books of our day which are worthy of the study of posterity" (6, 616). One must admit, he concludes, that lexicography is one area in which the moderns have surpassed the ancients.

The Academy grammar, to which Fénelon next refers, had been an even greater victim of time and indecision than the dictionary. In 1701, after much procrastination, the academicians relegated to the Abbé Régnier-Desmarais the task of preparing such a book. When he presented the group with his *Traité de la grammaire française (Treatise on French Grammar)* in 1706, they promptly voiced their displeasure and refused to adopt it.[1] It was not, incredibly enough, until 1932 that the Académie Française published its *Grammaire*. Even then the project, said largely to be the work of Abel Hermant, provoked a fair amount of hostile criticism, notably the *Observations sur la Grammaire de l'Académie Française (Observations on the Grammar of the French Academy)* by Ferdinand Brunot.

Fénelon does not allude to Desmarais' treatise; he simply voices the opinion that the dictionary should be supplemented by a grammar. In turn he mentions again the usefulness of such a work for foreigners studying the French language. Beyond that, Frenchmen themselves might need to consult grammatical rules; after all, they have learned their language through speaking it, and usage alone is not completely trustworthy. "Each province," Fénelon observes, "has its own incorrect manner of speech, even Paris" (6, 616). Like the Greeks and Romans, he asserts, it will behoove his compatriots to read and study the grammarians so that they may observe such things as rules, exception to the rules, etymologies, and the subtleties of the language.

As for the actual composition of the grammar, Fénelon advocates what he terms "a short and easy method" (6, 616). He therefore issues a warning against too great a display of learning. In phrases that recall the precepts of his *Traité de l'éducation des filles,* he encourages the author of such a book to make his rules as general as possible, dealing with exceptions as they arise. The principal idea is to acquaint the reader as quickly as possible with "the sensible application of rules through frequent usage" (6, 616). Afterwards, he can delve into those linguistic intricacies of which he was at first unaware. In concluding, Fénelon notes that a grammarian cannot expect to hold a living language within fixed and limited barriers. His work can, however, impose a certain restriction on "capricious changes" which are so evident in the area of fashion; language should be perfected, not muddled and altered to suit the desires of "pure whim" (6, 616).

II *Fénelon and the French Language*

If in his section on the Academy grammar Fénelon had left with the reader any image or impression of conservatism with regard to language, he seems inclined in the next part of his *Lettre,* entitled "A Plan for the Enrichment of the Language," to dispel such a notion. At the outset he declares quite bluntly that for at least a century the purists have kept the French language in a state of impoverishment and constraint, and that as a result it "lacks a goodly number of words and phrases" (6, 616). This necessitous condition causes him to think back with a certain nostalgia to the conciseness, ingenuousness, boldness, and forcefulness of "the old language" exemplified in his mind by such sixteenth-century writers as Marot, Amyot, and Cardinal d'Ossot. Much like La Bruyère (in the section "De Quelques Usages" of *Les Caractères*), Fénelon would like to reclaim many of the outmoded words that had through the years gradually been cast aside.

Fénelon's notions about the French language are not limited to sentimental musings about the past. He advocates some definite measures aimed at embellishing his native tongue: the adoption of compound words in the manner of the Greeks and Romans, the appropriation of dialect words which would be particularly useful in creating more varied and pliable versification, and the use of foreign terms. Words, according to Fénelon, are only arbitrary sounds or symbols by means of which one communicates; isolated, they therefore have no particular value. Most of all, one must remember that they belong just as much to those who borrow them as to those who lend them. "Let us take from all quarters," he advises, "everything we need to render our language clearer and more precise. Any sort of circumlocution weakens discourse" (6, 617).

Fénelon realizes, of course, that his plan may indeed be a dangerous one. So it is that he formulates the conditions that should govern the fortification and enrichment of the language. The task of choosing new terms and expressions should be left to "people of a proven taste and discernment," and not to the "unknowing rabble" or the "fashionable dictates of women" ("au vulgaire ignorant ou à la mode des femmes" 6, 617). He seems to retreat to some degree from his implied policy of indiscriminate borrowing of foreign terms by cautioning against the danger of making French "a shapeless, crude accumulation of other languages" (6, 617). In this respect, the Academy can play an important role, as can "people with the greatest reputation for good taste" (6, 618).

This part of the Lettre may very well be considered the most chimerical, the most highly fanciful of any of its sections. His mind, reaching into those areas that he more than likely considered bold and innovative, seems unable to grasp fully the idea that language, although made for man, is created by a long and natural process; and that academies and other arbiters, no matter how refined and cultured they may be, cannot expect to exert the necessary controls over so liberal a program as he proposes.[2] Fénelon seems to have forgotten that his plan resembles in many ways the basically unsuccessful goals of Du Bellay, Ronsard, and the Pléiade poets of the sixteenth century. In short, Fénelon gives the distinct impression that he is trying to be, as he will remain throughout most of the Lettre, both ancient and modern: reactionary, he praises the Greeks and Romans for certain aspects of their vocabulary; progressive, he flaunts before the purists of his time his imaginative spirit of reform.[3]

III   *Rhetoric*

Fénelon's ideas on rhetoric in the *Lettre* are largely reiterative of those he had expressed much earlier in the *Dialogues sur l'élo-quence*. The reader quickly discerns that the three or so decades that separate the two works have produced no critical fluctuation: the proposals of the *Lettre* are but a further affirmation of his belief that true eloquence is free of ostentation, ornamentation, and trick-ery. With as much vehemence as in the *Dialogues*, Fénelon pro-claims his contempt for the orator, either secular or sacred, who sacrifices truth and righteousness for the sake of brilliance and van-ity. For him such a man is nothing more than "a professional hawker who uses his words as a charlatan does to sell his cures" (6, 622).

Certain features, however, distinguish this section on rhetoric from the *Dialogues*. Besides the clarification and extension of his previous remarks concerning order and arrangement, the most no-table addition in the *Lettre* is the relation of the question of rhetoric to the Quarrel of the Ancients and the Moderns. Drawing upon Fontenelle's comparison in defense of the Moderns, Fénelon asserts that he has no doubt that men, like trees which attain the same size and bear the same fruit as they did two thousand years ago, are capable of equalling their forerunners. But he proposes, all the same, two qualifications with regard to this observation: first, one must take into account the effect of climate, since Languedoc and Provence, for example, produce grapes and figs of a more delicate taste than Normandy and the Low Countries. Likewise, one can say that by nature the Arcadians were more naturally suited to the cultivation of the fine arts than the Scythians; and the Sicilians are more musically inclined than the Laplanders. Secondly, Fénelon calls attention to the long tradition and high respect for eloquence in Greece. The spoken word, which wielded such great influence on the social and political activity of that nation, has never held a place of equal importance in France. The art of eloquence, he maintains, is limited at the present time to the law courts where the advocate, eager to reason clearly and win his case, is little interested in in-spiring words; and to the pulpit where the preacher, often a young man, is more concerned with his own reputation than with the salvation of souls.

Fénelon's chapter on rhetoric stands then as his final sally against the oratorical practices of his day. Spokesman for "the rapid simplicity" of Demosthenes, he remains no less the champion of eloquence, which he conceives of as a moral and impassioned art "destined to instruct, to repress the passions, to correct man's behavior, to uphold the laws, to conduct public deliberations, to make men good and happy" (6, 622).

IV *Fénelon's Poetics*

Since the Academy was still considering the formulation of a poetics, Fénelon judges it appropriate here in the *Lettre* to endorse such an undertaking and then to draft some of his reflections about the nature of poetry. After defending the seriousness and utility of the genre, whose civilizing and religious role he traces in rapid fashion, he launches into an attack against the disadvantages and weaknesses of French versification. In his letter of January 26, 1714, to La Motte, Fénelon had already censured what he termed "the severity of the rules" affecting French prosody. Here in this section of the *Lettre* he repeats with greater amplification much of what he had already stated: that rhyme is more of a hindrance than an asset; that it causes the poet to overcharge his work with forced epithets and needless lines, thereby creating inharmonious, dull, and sluggish verses. Fénelon, on the other hand, is quite aware that the abolishment of rhyme would be an impossibility; it is a sort of necessary evil, but one that can be tolerated if the poet is allowed more freedom in the use of rhyme. With this greater leeway, he would be capable of achieving a meaning that would be both more precise and more harmonious.

To liberate French versification to an even greater degree, Fénelon next advocates (he intimates as much in the letter to La Motte cited above) the use of inversion, which, as he illustrates with quotations from Virgil's seventh and eighth *Eclogues* and a Horatian ode (IV, 4), furnished the ancient poets their majesty, grace, and harmony. Inversion, however, Fénelon cautions, is a poetic technique that must be utilized sparingly. The poet Pierre de Ronsard (1524–85), in spite of his innovative attempts to enrich the French language, carried it too far and ended by speaking "French in Greek" (6, 627). Above all, clarity and precision must not be sacrificed, unless, of course, the writer has the intention of composing riddles. Excessive delicacy degenerates into subtle and obscure language which only confuses the reader.

At this point Fénelon, as he had done in his *Discours de réception* à *l'Académie Française* (1693) and will do later in the section on the Ancients and the Moderns, relates poetry to architecture. Condemning hyperbolic diction and unnecessary ornamentation, he envisions a literary work as an edifice that possesses no decoration simply for the sake of decoration. Naturalness, the great leitmotiv of his aesthetic, is heard again and with it a stern disapproval for those authors who try to dazzle and impress their readers. "I like a man," says Fénelon, "who makes me forget he is a writer, who puts himself on an equal footing with me, just as if we were engaged in a conversation" (6, 628). Once more, almost as an unconditioned reflex, he equates the word *natural* with *nature* itself: instead of summoning forth his wit and his cleverness, the author, in Fénelon's estimation, should show "a farmer who fears for his harvest, a shepherd who knows nothing except his village and his flock, a nurse full of concern for her little one" (6, 628). Fénelon's love of rustic, simple things has not diminished; as in the past, he much prefers a graceful pastoral setting to brilliant inventions, the quiet and naive descriptions of a Virgil or a Horace. Beauty, as Fénelon emphasizes, "is so natural a thing that it has by way of novelty no need of catching me unawares" (6, 629).

In the concluding pages of this section, where he does little more than continue his plea for naturalness, Fénelon defines poetry as "an imitation and a painting" (6, 629). For him this means that the poet, like artists such as Raphael and Titian, attempts not to startle or bedazzle the viewer with bizarre or grotesque elements, but rather to achieve truth through resemblance or likeness. By following this precept his creative force will be led to depict, as Homer sometimes does, unaffected and artless details from everyday life. Thus Fénelon admits (and it comes as no surprise) his taste for "this simplicity of mores" which "seems to bring back the Golden Age" (6, 629). In rejecting such *précieux* novels as Madeleine de Scudéry's *Clélie* (1654–60) and La Calprenède's *Cléopâtre* (1647–56)—to which, incidentally, he specifically refers—he underlines his scorn for the false and the tasteless; in very precise terms he informs the Moderns (Charles Perrault, for example, had highly praised the novels just cited) that he cannot accept their insipid heroes. What Fénelon exhorts the poet to imitate is the passion and the truth, as well as the grief and solitude, of Virgil, Horace, and Catullus (though Fénelon is shocked by the latter's obscenities). Embracing completely the idea of "passionate simplicity," he ends his section on poetry with the following lines: "Beauty which is only beautiful, that is to say brilliant, is only partly beautiful; one must express the passions in order to inspire them; one must seize the heart in order to direct it toward the legitimate goal of a poem" (6, 633).

As much as any part of the *Lettre*, Fénelon's ideas on poetry stand as proof of his determination to remain free and independent of literary schools and factions. While it is true that his attack on French versification clearly anticipates the tenets that La Motte and other Moderns will espouse soon afterwards; and though it is evident that his ideas about the relationship of the arts reflect the theories of Perrault, Fénelon's refusal to repudiate Homer and ancient simplicity clearly marks his disavowal of modern refinement and sophistication. His unwavering attachment to naturalness is in the final analysis perhaps his greatest source of originality in the section: it is his great link to Rousseau and the notion of man's noble and primitive heritage. It is indeed a very short step from Fénelon's evocation of the grief and tenderness of poetry to the sentimental ruminations of Jean-Jacques and the Romantic generation of 1820. Consciously united to the past, he unconsciously blazes a trail for a literature of sensibility and freedom.

V *Tragedy*

Fénelon begins his section on tragedy by establishing its clear-cut separation from comedy and by defining it as the representation of "great events which arouse violent passions" (6, 633). This statement leads him immediately to an attack against those who, ignoring ancient concepts, have made tragedy a weak, colorless, insipid genre, dependent for its effect on "this inconstant and disordered love which wreaks so much havoc" (6, 633). It is the absence of the love element which accounts in part for the superiority of Greek tragedy. Even Corneille and Racine, the two French tragic poets who, in Fénelon's estimation, deserve the greatest praise (they are also the only ones to whom he alludes), were guilty of surrendering to this taste for what he terms "romantic plays" (*pièces romanesques*). As examples he cites the Dircé-Thésée episode in Corneille's *Oedipe* and the Hippolyte-Aricie love interest in Racine's *Phèdre*. If Racine's heroine had been left alone in all her rage, she would have transformed the action of that play into something that was "unique, short, lively, and rapid" (6, 633).

Besides the "gallant intrigue" other abuses call for remedy. The epigrammatic speeches of tragedy, for example, are pompous and affected; passion, grief, and despair have in certain instances become contrived and flowery instead of noble and intense. Natural speech is what the tragic genre should possess, and a long recitation such as Théramène's narrative in *Phèdre* (V, 6) is illustrative of what Fénelon calls "misplaced elegance" (6, 634); for him it is a far cry from the broken, uninterrupted lines of Sophocles' *Oedipus* who speaks with the voice of nature "when she succumbs to grief" (6, 634). Faithful to his aesthetic canon, Fénelon couples with naturalness the idea of simplicity. Once more, as in the section on poetry, he speaks of the handicaps of rhyme which have led the French poet to write unnatural-sounding lines far removed from the serious, noble, and passionate speech one might generally expect. As Fénelon reminds his reader, "The more one depicts great characters and strong passions, the more necessary it is to write with a noble and vehement simplicity" (6, 635). In this respect he finds that Corneille fell far short of the mark; the Augustus of *Cinna*, for example, with his grandiloquent diction, stands in marked contrast to that same emperor who is portrayed with "modest simplicity" by Suetonius (6, 635). The Roman should be depicted as lofty and great, but he should also be revealed—in the manner of Cicero, Livy, and Plutarch—as a man who was natural and restrained in his speech.

Fénelon's condemnation of the langorous and weak aspect of French tragedy presented the reader with no new or revolutionary concept. In the ninth of his *Satires*, Boileau, although more receptive to the use of the love element, had already ridiculed the cold, passionless, and artificial approach to tragedy. On the other hand, Fénelon's attack on rhyme and his statements concerning verbosity and pompousness in tragedy are not to be accepted as common for the era. Much of what he says in this regard anticipates the theories that will be expounded soon after, for example, by La Motte and Du Bos, and then later in the century by Diderot, Mercier, and La Harpe. Fénelon also has the somewhat dubious honor of being perhaps the first or one of the first to criticize negatively the now-famous Théramène *récit*. His reaction to the author of *Phèdre* leaves us an impression of severity, but only an impression: Fénelon somehow seems aware that Racine had achieved to some degree Sophocles' "forceful and simple sorrow" (6, 634), and basically he is more favorable to him than to Corneille.

VI *Comedy*

Fully aware that comedy is a dramatic form which speaks "in a less lofty tone than tragedy" (6, 636), Fénelon nevertheless censures those playwrights who allowed their work to take on the elements of low comedy and vulgar farce. In rejecting the likes of Aristophanes and Plautus (specifically mentioned), he turns to his ideal representative of the genre, Terence, praising him for his "inimitable naiveté" (6, 636) and his "simple and touching words" (6, 637). This evaluation, nothing short of a tribute, is abruptly followed by his consideration of Molière, who, as he concedes, is "a great comic poet" (6, 637). Molière is remarkable, in fact, for having delved further into character study than Terence; and, in this respect, Fénelon chooses to speak of him as a sort of pioneer ("Everything considered, Molière blazed a completely new trail," 6, 637). He is, however, in our critic's estimation, an author not without defects: one finds in Molière's plays, for example, a forced and unnatural style ("Terence says in four words with the most elegant simplicity what Molière could only state with a multitude of metaphors," 6, 637), an exaggerated characterization, and a depiction of vice as pleasing and virtue as ridiculous and odious. He also hazards the opinion that Molière, cramped by French versification, wrote better prose than poetry; and that in *Amphitryon*, "where he took the liberty of composing irregular verse" (*vers libres* or lines of irregular length), he was far more successful than in the comedies written entirely in alexandrines. In the final paragraph, almost an echo of the opening section in which he decries the unrefined elements of comedy, Fénelon, alluding to Boileau's lines from the *Art poétique* (III, 399–400), reprimands the author of *Le Misanthrope* for having stooped so low as to borrow the devices (he says specifically "the banter," 6, 638) of the Italian players.

In his discussion of comedy Fénelon refers to no contemporary playwright other than Molière. The emphasis that he places on explicating the force and beauty of Terence's work clearly identifies him as a partisan of the Ancients. At the same time, his preference for Terence over Plautus indicates, to my mind, a sort of double vision. First of all, most cultivated Frenchmen of Fénelon's time— and I base this statement in part on the large number of editions and translations printed in France between 1614 and 1716—would probably have shown a marked predilection for the author of the

Andria.[4] Fénelon, in repudiating broad, unsophisticated comedy, therefore speaks, not only in the manner of a priest, but also, like Boileau, as a man of taste and refinement. Secondly, Fénelon's recognition of those touching, tender, and moving lines of the *Andria* (6, 637) establishes him as an early precursor of Diderot, who will discover in Terence a noteworthy ancestor of the sentimental, tearful drama of eighteenth-century France.

Although an Ancient in taste and a Modern in spirit, Fénelon is, with regard to Molière, no less the churchman. When he turns to a consideration of virtue and vice in that playwright, he may well avoid the harsh and biting tone of Bossuet's remarks to Father Caffaro in the *Maximes et réflexions sur la comédie* (*Maxims and Reflections on Comedy*, 1694); but he relays, nonetheless, the tempered lesson of the ever-alert moralizer. His view looks ahead to Rousseau's less gracious evaluation of Molière in the *Lettre à D'Alembert sur les spectacles* (*Letter to D'Alembert on the Public Stage*, 1758).

VII *History and the Historian*

A treatise on history did not figure among the Academy's projects, but Fénelon's advocacy of such a work gave him an obviously welcome pretext to discuss a subject area which had long interested him. Sometime, probably before 1689, most likely at the behest of the Duc de Beauvillier, he had composed for that nobleman's two sons an *Histoire de Charlemagne*. This manuscript, never published, was presumably burned in a fire which partially destroyed the archbishopric palace at Cambrai in 1697; but Fénelon's letter to Beauvillier concerning that work (7, 213) constitutes a sort of preamble to the discussion contained in the *Lettre à l'Académie*. His concern for history is further borne out by his placing great emphasis on a discipline that he regarded as an essential part of the curriculum of the Duc de Bourgogne, and by the *Dialogues des morts*, described by a modern editor of Fénelon as "a sort of dramatic review of universal history."[5]

It is not surprising, then, given Fénelon's pedagogical identification with the genre, that he begins his consideration of history in the *Lettre à l'Académie* by affirming its moral and political significance. Like Cicero in the *De Oratore* and Bossuet in the *Discours sur l'histoire universelle* (*Discourse on Universal History*), he sees history as the mirror of great example as well as a school for those who would learn of wicked men's vices; a device for teaching us "by what pathway mankind has passed from one form of government to another" (6, 638). From this concept he leaps in rapid fashion to explain the requisites of the historian himself: impartial and neutral, he avoids panegyrics as well as satire in order to concentrate on the objective treatment of historical figures; sober and discreet, he shuns a display of erudition and refrains from furnishing his reader "dry and detached" facts of "superfluous" incidents (6, 638). Fénelon prefers, in fact, an inexact historian to one who deals only in names and what he calls "sterile dates" (6, 638). In this respect, he praises the fourteenth-century historian Froissart for his natural, vivid depiction of detail.

This idea of movement and realism is of equal importance with Fénelon's recommendation of order and arrangement. To achieve these qualities he requires that the historian view his work in a unified manner ("comme d'une seule vue," 6, 639), or as Arthur Tilley interprets this phrase, as "a continuous chain of cause and effect."[6] This does not mean that this type of unity relies on chronology alone; for, according to Fénelon, an historian of true genius will choose from many the one location where a fact can most advantageously be used; where, in the final analysis, "it will throw light on all the others" (6, 639). True order also involves the use of a clear, pure, and precise diction—the *pura et illustri brevitate* (elegant and luminous brevity) proclaimed by Cicero—which shows no ornamentation, but rather exhibits what Fénelon terms "this nudity which is so noble and majestic" (6, 639).

More significant than these rhetorical considerations in Fénelon's estimation is the careful, faithful reproduction of background details which reveal the mores of a given nation in a given century. He therefore urges the historian to think in accurate terms so that he may avert the errors evidenced by the artists of the Lombard school (he could just as well have said the Venetian school) who ignored any sort of authenticity in the depiction of what he terms *il costume* (historical or local color). Clovis' court, for example, should not be described as either polite or magnificent, for, after all, those ancient Gauls were nothing more than barbarians. In similar fashion, the historian, knowledgeable with regard to the changes in the form of government, should be able to discuss the evolution of political institutions; as Fénelon concludes, "It is a hundred times more important to observe these changes in an entire nation than simply to record isolated facts" (6, 640).

Having thus outlined his standards for the "excellent historian," Fénelon in turn admits that such a person "is perhaps even more rare than a great poet" (6, 640). To demonstrate what he means, he concludes this section by summoning forth the notable and representative names of the genre and evaluating their contributions. His rapid survey, which begins with Herodotus (perfect so far as narrative power, but a failure when it came to writing a unified, well-ordered history), embraces, among others, Xenophon (the *Cyropaedia* is more a philosophical novel than a history), Thucydides (guilty of making up the speeches of his historical personages), and Tacitus (he shows much genius, but his work displays too much art, too much refinement, and all in all too much "mysterious brevity," 6, 641). For his final example he chooses the sixteenth-century historian Davila, whom Fénelon finds pleasurable to read despite the fact that "he speaks as if he had been party to the most secret of councils" (6, 641).

Critics such as Janet have spoken with great affirmation of the originality of this section on history.[7] Although, along with Fleury, Fénelon may well have been the first to apply the notion of accuracy in local and historical color to this particular genre (Boileau had already insisted on this principle with regard to literature); and although he speaks with a modern voice in proclaiming the need for the historian to know and record the evolutionary changes in institutions and mores, he was nonetheless indebted for many of his ideas to authors both ancient and contemporary: to Cicero as well as Pellisson for his ideas on clarity of diction, to Horace and Father Daniel for their views concerning order and arrangement, and to Lucian for his view of the impartial historian.[8] Fénelon does not allude to Bossuet—or to any other seventeenth-century historian for that matter—but his attitude toward the moral implications of history closely parallels the tenets expressed by that prelate in his *Discours sur l'histoire universelle*.

I have no doubt that Fénelon should be considered a precursor to later historians—Voltaire, as well as François Guizot, Adolphe Thiers, and Augustin Thierry; what should be elucidated, however, (as Cahen does) is that Fénelon's role as historical theorist passed for all intents and purposes unnoticed.[9] When, for example, Thierry in his *Récits des temps mérovingiens* (1840) speaks of his inspiration with regard to the color and animation of his narrative, he salutes Chateaubriand, not Fénelon, as his master and guide. As in the case of the *Dialogues sur l'éloquence,* Fénelon has perhaps not received his full due as innovator and critic. His modern, enlightened approach to history, spiced with his impressionistic view of "superstitious exactitude" (6, 638), points us toward the natural, well-organized but imaginative historian.

VIII   *The Ancients and the Moderns*

Ever since the Renaissance the writer and artist had accepted the more or less unquestionable superiority of the Greeks and Romans in matters of inspiration and imitation. In seventeenth-century France, however, the adherents of classicism, heirs to the cult for ancient models, began to be challenged by a new spirit of reaction and reform. In the earlier part of the century, such writers as Theophile de Viau, Charles Sorel, and Saint-Amant sought to defend, either through critical prefaces or the works themselves, the right of the artist to independence and liberty. What in some ways may have been an underground movement turned into a more overt rebellion when Desmarets de Saint-Sorlin, among others, chose to write epic poems treating Christian themes and figures. When his *Clovis* (1657) and his *Esther* (1673) were attacked by Boileau in Canto III of his *Art poétique (Art of Poetry),* Desmarets responded with a *Défense de la poésie et de la langue française (Defense of Poetry and the French Language,* 1675), his bid to demonstrate the superiority of the Christian marvellous over the pagan.

The second phase of the Quarrel, conducted with more vigor by a great cast of participants, began early in 1687. In January of that year Charles Perrault read before the Académie Française his poem *Le Siècle de Louis le Grand,* a composition designed to extol the writers and philosophers of his century at the expense of the revered Ancients. Once more Boileau jumped into the fray, joined by other defenders of classicism, most notably La Fontaine and La Bruyère. Perrault formed his army of Moderns, enlisting the aid of Fontenelle. In 1688 the latter published his *Digression sur les Anciens et les Modernes (Digression on the Ancients and the Moderns),* a work that led the Quarrel into the realm of science by linking the superiority of the age of Louis XIV to the concept of a transmission of cumulative knowledge and to the idea of progress. In the matter of literature and the arts, Fontenelle struck a compromise, however, for he maintained that in those areas the Moderns could at least equal the Ancients. The same year of the *Digression* Perrault further defended his group with the first of his *Parallèles des Anciens et des Modernes (Parallel of the Ancients and the Moderns)*, which vaunted among other things the more accurate psychology employed by contemporary writers. A certain wave of intellectual opinion favoring these new ideas swept the Moderns to victory: in 1691 Fontenelle was elected to the Academy. Throughout the next few years, at least until 1694, the controversy dragged along, with Boileau playing an active role as defender of the Ancients. By 1700, however, the Quarrel had lost a good deal of its vitality; and the author of the *Art poétique*, in an effort at reconciliation, wrote to Perrault, admitting that there were indeed excellent modern writers, and that Louis XIV's century was certainly equal to that of Augustus.

The peaceful settlement between the factions was only a superficial and transitory one. In 1713 the so-called third phase of the Quarrel—and the one which was to involve Fénelon—broke out again. This new outburst was sparked by the publication of Houdar de la Motte's far from faithful rendering of *The Iliad*, a poetic version which counted among its features the reduction of the number of cantos from twenty-four to twelve. Unable to read Greek, La Motte had relied on the scholarly translation of Madame Dacier (1699; second edition, 1718). Upon reading the new version, and being particularly incensed by the prefatory discourse on Homer, the learned lady attacked La Motte's efforts in a long pamphlet entitled *Des causes de la corruption du goût (On the Causes for the Corruption in Taste*, 1714). His reply, the *Réflexions sur la critique*, rallied other Moderns to his side. The Abbé d'Aubignac, for one, in his *Conjectures académiques (Academic Conjectures)* went so far as to challenge the existence of Homer.[10]

Fénelon was gradually drawn into the dispute through his correspondence with La Motte. In his letter of January 26, 1714, which contains his polite and subtle criticism of the latter's *Iliad*, he alludes to the Quarrel as "this Parnassian civil war" (6, 651). At the same time Fénelon reveals his intention to remain impartial; and it is therefore not surprising that, when later that year he includes a section on the Ancients and Moderns in his letter to the Academy, he exhibits a conciliatory, arbitrational attitude with regard to the argument. He seems determined not to offend the Moderns, or at least to allay their fears lest they think him a fanatic classicist. Fénelon thus expresses the hope that "the Moderns will surpass the

Ancients," and that in his century there will be "poets more sublime than Homer" (6, 641). The date of a work, he continues, has nothing to do with judging a work. Contemporary writers must look ahead to the pathway that has been cleared for them by great writers who preceded them in time and achievement.

While giving hope, then, to those who might think it impossible to equal the Ancients, Fénelon nevertheless speaks out against the Moderns' scorn and neglect of the great writers of antiquity. Like Horace, whose *De Arte Poetica* he quotes, and like Du Bellay, the Pléiade theorist, he advises the writers of his century to read and consult the Greek and Latin models, to follow even more closely than they did the imitation of *la belle nature*. By that Fénelon (although he does not explain the term) means not an adherence to pure nature, wild and disordered, but an imitation of an ideal one which aims for artistic perfection.[11] The modern writer must also be careful not to overestimate his creation; he should learn to resist the overenthusiastic evaluations of his friends. After all, he reminds the presumptuous writer, "Nothing here on earth is entirely perfect" (6, 643).

After positing this rather forbidding declaration, Fénelon apparently feels the need once more to put the Moderns at ease. To demonstrate his unprejudiced attitude he is prepared to discuss the imperfections of the Ancients. He therefore willingly admits, quoting Horace, that Homer "nodded a bit sometimes in a long poem" (6, 643); that the chorus of the ancient tragedy often interrupted the action with vague and meaningless discourses, and that the great Cicero was guilty of cold witticisms, needless puns, and the most ridiculous sort of vanity. Even Horace, who is unquestionably one of Fénelon's preferred authors, is by no means exempt from flaws. Generally speaking, for Fénelon there is in the background of the Ancients' work that one great basis of inferiority, and it is to be explained in terms of "the defect of their religion and the coarseness of their philosophy" (6, 644).

Given these pronouncements, Fénelon at this point realizes that he has come dangerously close to tipping the scales in the direction of the Moderns. He therefore ends his discussion with a consideration of the superior quality of the Ancients. Although they have bequeathed to us, he maintains, very few truly excellent books, the authors of antiquity "have given us almost all the best of what we have . . ." (6, 645). Their works may contain a number of careless

expressions, just as the great painters sometimes reveal certain neg-
ligible features, but the judicious critic is quick to realize that a
displaced work or a slipshod phrase destroys neither the beauty of
the whole nor the order and power which are everywhere present.
Most of all, Fénelon praises what he has praised before—"that ancient simplicity," that "happy and elegant simplicity" which scorned
"vain and ruinous luxury" (6, 646). Once more, as in the section on
poetry, Fénelon casts still another nostalgic glance backwards to a
time when the world was still happy enough to be unaware of the
"monstrous mores" of the modern age (6, 646). Once more he voices
his dislike of ornamentation and, as an echo of the *Dialogues sur
l'éloquence*, condemns the Gothic style:

. . . A Greek building has no ornament which is there merely for the sake of
ornamentation; the parts necessary to support it or cover it such as columns
and cornices are turned into graceful beauty through their proportions.
Everything is simple and restrained and limited to playing a useful
part . . . Gothic architecture, on the other hand, elevates upon very slen-
der pillars an immense vaulted roof which reaches into the sky. One would
think that it is going to fall, despite the fact that it has lasted for centuries. It
is full of windows, rose-windows, and pointed pinnacles. Its stone seems to
be cut like cardboard. Everything is open and airy . . . (6, 648).

Gothic architecture, as Fénelon reminds his readers, was regarded
by its creators as a refinement which surpassed the simplicity of the
Greek style. Like architects, he surmises, poets and orators have
believed through the years that they were superior to their predecessors; how mistaken, however, they were to think in that fashion. Contemporary authors, he concludes, should fear the same
deception.
    Thus Fénelon's oscillatory technique leads him to the point where
a final decision is expected. Quoting Virgil's third *Eclogue*, he ends
his commentary by confirming his neutrality and by awarding the
prize to both the new and the old. The result was that La Motte, in
his letter to Fénelon of November 3, 1714, expressed great pleasure
with regard to the latter's conclusions about the Ancients and the
Moderns. Here was a statement written with such impartiality, with
such inconclusiveness in effect, that either faction in the Quarrel, as
La Motte himself pointed out, could easily claim Fénelon as a faithful partisan. Modern readers have wondered, and rightly so, about

Fénelon's true intent. Did La Motte, for example, really fail to notice that whenever Fénelon needs to support a theory or an idea, he almost invariably has recourse to a quotation from an ancient author; and that in the final analysis, he cites only two Moderns (Malherbe and Racan)? Were readers on either side of the Quarrel aware that despite his unfavorable comments about Aristophanes, Ovid, Lucan, Plautus, and Seneca, he displays a love for Virgil, Horace, and Homer which has only deepened through the years? Perhaps it is wiser to conclude that Fénelon in his polite and restrained manner is neither insincere nor equivocal. Rather let it be said that his taste for ancient letters, so blatantly evident, has not diminished; it has simply become more selective.[12] Fully prepared to reject any foolish, superstitious attachment to the past, Fénelon looks to a future that is capable of upholding nature and beauty, those principles of which he is truly the stalwart champion

IX   Evaluation

Not only does the Lettre à l'Académie rank among Fénelon's better-known works, but it is also the one that has received the most effusive praise. As difficult as it may be to accept critic George Saintbury's rather categorical opinion that it is "the most valuable single piece of criticism that France had yet produced,"[13] it is well to remember the appraisal of other critics, Gustave Lanson, Albert Schinz, and Alfred Lombard among them, who judge the Lettre, aside from Boileau's Art poétique, as the most important and significant of French critical documents.[14] It comes, then, as something of a surprise to read Lemaître's somewhat pejorative description of the work as "a pleasant chat . . . almost the comfortable chattering of an old man steeped in classic antiquity."[15] Lemaître's view of the impressionistic quality of the work as its most remarkable characteristic does serve to remind us, however, that the Lettre is really only a prelude to a poetics which, if written, might have indeed been filled with stunning and innovative ideas.

Such a view need not convince us that the Lettre is by any means banal and ineffective. In the background of Fénelon's fleeting and sometime chimerical remarks exist "solid thought, decided principles, and a taste which is sure of itself."[16] Although Fénelon's critical stance may well recall Boileau's, Fénelon's is almost completely free of dogmatism and therefore more inclined toward flexibility. Most of all, it is well to remember that the simple nature of Fénelon, unlike that of Boileau and the classical school, is "more unadorned, more perfectly pure, less subjected to the concern for order and grandeur."[17] Reflective of a mind that is completely open to new ideas and filled with what one critic has called the eighteenth-century "idea of perfectability,"[18] the *Lettre* is truly a document of the transition; by displaying an attitude that is never completely dominated by either an extreme rationality or a crushing wave of sensibility, Fénelon has left behind an image of the orderly, amiable critic in search of beauty and simplicity.

Conclusion

Even in times like these, when demythification is a favorite pastime, it is not easy to liberate a figure like Fénelon from a disturbing maze of controversy and legend. For some, he will always remain a neurasthenic whose spiritual meanderings led him into the rarefied atmosphere of "pure love." For others, forgetful of his aristocratic temperament and his unwavering loyalty to Catholic doctrine, he will forever bear the label of charitable and tolerant precursor of the Enlightenment. Each generation will, of course, continue to exercise its right to discover Fénelon the man and to reexamine his works. Consciously or unconsciously, however, the literary critic, the historian, or the psychologist of any age will have to face the undeniable fact that he is indeed a complex personality.

The complicated aspects of Fénelon's character and disposition need not, on the other hand, obscure the fact that his work and thought exemplify well the spirit of his age. Running throughout his writings—from the *Dialogues sur l'éloquence* to the *Lettre à l'Académie*—are the guiding principles of simplicity and naturalness; they are, all told, his major links to that movement we so conveniently call classicism and to the humanistic currents of his time. Except perhaps for Racine, there is no other seventeenth-century French writer who so thoroughly cultivated the Ancients, or who was more successful in translating the spirit and vigor of the antique world into a context tinged with Christian melancholy. Unlike the author of *Phèdre*, however, Fénelon never quite managed to infuse his work with a sense of the universal. This shortcoming is most evident in *Télémaque*, where the author's pagan, sensual grace is quite heavily shadowed by his moral purpose and didactic aims.

Fénelon's vision of a serene, Virgilian Golden Age, rather than casting him back into a hermetic fantasy world of chimera and self-indulgent dreams, had, in fact, the opposite effect. It must surely be looked on as a major factor in the development of his *crise de conscience*. Unable to remain silent in the face of social and economic abuses, especially from 1690 on, Fénelon transformed the outlines of his dreams and aspirations into political statements which reflect the malaise and dissatisfaction prevalent during the latter part of Louis XIV's reign. We are therefore entitled to study Fénelon as an enlightened thinker, but we must remember that as priest and moralist, he consistently subordinated his theories to the demands of a Christian and a Catholic doctrine.

As orthodox, both theologically and artistically, as he was, Fénelon never allowed his spirit to be held within the confines of an overpowering rigidity. His attraction to the mystic doctrine of Madame Guyon illustrated his tendency to seek that region where the brightness of sensibility and emotion replace, for at least a while, the threatening gloom of a cold and depressing lassitude. In the areas of literature and aesthetics as well, he demonstrated an affinity for innovative thought and freedom of expression. The *Lettre à l'Académie*, in many ways one of his greatest achievements, breathes as much as anything he wrote the spirit and reform of a new age. Imbued with a sense of history, an awareness of local color, and a love for sentiment, it points us toward the more daring reforms of the nineteenth century.

Fénelon is therefore both Ancient and Modern, a man whose life and works constitute a fascinating if not disturbing paradox. He may never rank among the greatest writers of seventeenth-century France, for he does not possess, for example, the artistry of La Fontaine, the true genius of Pascal, or the diversity of La Bruyère and La Rochefoucauld. Whether or not Fénelon deserves to be studied more as a personality than a writer is an issue that cannot be settled here. Whatever approach we might prefer to take, however, it would be unfortunate to minimize the influence of his ideas, his prose style, and the power of his imagination on the growth and development of French literature.

Notes and References

Chapter One

1. *Correspondance de Fénelon*, ed. Jean Orcibal (Paris: Klincksieck, 1972–76) I, 23. Hereafter referred to as Orcibal.

2. Jeanne-Lydie Goré, *L'Itinéraire de Fénelon: Humanisme et spiritualité* (Paris: Presses Universitaires de France, 1957), p. 52. Hereafter cited as Goré, *L'Itinéraire.*

3. The translation is by W. H. Jervis and is cited by H. C. Barnard in his *Fénelon on Education* (Cambridge: The University Press, 1966), p. ix. Hereafter referred to as Barnard.

4. Orcibal, II, 49.

5. Albert Cherel, *Fénelon ou la religion du pur amour* (Paris: Denoël et Steele, 1934), p. 18. Hereafter cited as Cherel, *Fénelon ou la religion.*

6. *L'Intolérance de Fénelon* (Paris: Sandoz et Fischbacher, 1874).

7. Orcibal, I, 155–56.

8. The letter is dated January 16, 1686. See Orcibal, II, 20.

9. Orcibal, II, 31.

10. Ibid., 34.

11. Ibid., 59.

12. George R. Havens, *The Age of Ideas* (New York: The Free Press, 1965), p. 51. Hereafter referred to as Havens.

13. For a discussion of the dating of the *Traité de l'existence de Dieu* see Ely Carcassonne, *État présent des travaux sur Fénelon* (Paris: Société d'Edition "Les Belles Lettres," 1939), pp. 22–23; and Goré, *L'Itinéraire,* p. 132.

14. Louis de Rouvroy, Duc de Saint-Simon, *Mémoires*, ed. A. de Bois-lisle (Paris: Hachette, 1879–1928), II, 338.

15. Louis Guerrier cites this remark from Madame Guyon's *Vie* in his *Madame Guyon. Sa Vie, sa doctrine et son influence* (1881; rpt. Geneva: Slatkine, 1971), p. 179. Hereafter referred to as Guerrier.

16. Orcibal, II, 88.

17. Michael de la Bedoyere. *The Archbishop and the Lady* (London: Collins, 1956), p. 66.

18. Cited by Jules Lemaître, *Fénelon* (Paris: Arthème Fayard, 1910), p. 211. Hereafter referred to as Lemaître.

19. See Cherel's discussion of this point in *Fénelon ou la religion*, p. 101.

20. Ely Carcassonne, *Fénelon, l'homme et l'oeuvre* (Paris: Hatier-Boivin, 1946), p. 51. Hereafter referred to as Carcassonne, *Fénelon*.

21. Orcibal, IV, 83.

22. Guerrier, p. 322.

23. Ibid., p. 323.

24. Lemaître, p. 251.

25. A. Gazier, *Mélanges de littérature et d'histoire* (Paris: Armand Colin, 1904), p. 149.

26. This figure is cited by Antoine Adam in his *Histoire de la littérature française au XVIIe siècle* (Paris: Del Duca, 1962–68), V, 169. Hereafter referred to as Adam.

27. Carcassonne, *Fénelon*, p. 95.

Chapter Two

1. See, for example, the remarks of Albert Cahen in his edition of *Les Aventures de Télémaque* (Paris: Hachette, 1927), I, LVIII (hereafter referred to as Cahen, *Télémaque)* and Arthur Tilley, *The Decline of the Age of Louis XIV* (1929; rpt. New York: Barnes and Noble, 1968), p. 295 (Hereafter cited as Tilley).

2. François Gaquère, *La Vie et les oeuvres de Claude Fleury* (Paris: J. de Gigord, 1925), p. 265.

3. See the introduction to Wilbur Samuel Howell's translation, *The Dialogues on Eloquence* (Princeton, N.J.: Princeton University Press, 1951), pp. 6–46. Hereafter referred to as Howell.

4. Lemaître, p. 28.

5. Howell, pp. 44–46.

6. Ibid., p. 44.

7. Paul Janet, *Fénelon* (Paris: Hachette, 1892), p. 176. Hereafter referred to as Janet. Cf. Goré, *L'Itinéraire*, p. 251; and Marguerite Haillant, *Fénelon et la prédication* (Paris: Klincksieck, 1969), p. 150. Hereafter referred to as Haillant.

8. Goré, *L'Itinéraire*, p. 252.

9. Henri Sy, "Le Séminaire des Missions Etrangères. Le Sermon de Fénelon sur la Vocation des Gentils," *Revue d'histoire des Missions*, septembre 1933, pp. 335–36. Sy proposes that the sermon was delivered in January, 1687.

10. Tilley, p. 301.

11. Lemaître, p. 25.

12. Haillant, p. 157.

13. The letter is dated December 28, 1685. See Orcibal, III, 53.

14. See Barnard, p. xxxi; and Albert Cherel, "La Pédagogie fénelonienne,

son originalité, son influence au XVIIIᵉ siècle," *Revue d'Histoire Littéraire de la France*, 25 (1918), pp. 518–20.

15. W. H. Lewis, *The Splendid Century* (New York: William Sloane Associates, 1954), p. 244. Hereafter cited as Lewis.

16. Lewis, p. 241.

17. Lemaître, pp. 87–88.

18. Cherel, "La Pédagogie fénelonienne," p. 531.

19. M. Matter, *Le Mysticisme en France au temps de Fénelon* (Paris: Didier, 1865), p. 57.

20. Carcassonne, *Fénelon*, p. 16.

21. Sainte-Beuve, *Port-Royal* (Paris: Gallimard, 1953–55), III, 340.

22. Goré, *L'Itinéraire*, p. 215; Léon Ollé-Laprune, *La Philosophie de Malebranche* (Paris: Librairie Philosophique de Ladrange, 1870), II, 70.

23. L. Crouslé, *Fénelon et Bossuet* (Paris: Champion, 1894–95), I, 49.

24. Lemaître, p. 48.

25. Moïse Cagnac, *Fénelon, apologiste de la foi* (Paris: De Gigord, 1917), p. 64.

26. M. Langlois, *Fénelon, Pages nouvelles pour servir à l'étude des origines du quiétisme avant 1694* (Paris: Desclée de Brouwer, 1934), p. 28.

27. Haillant, pp. 16–18.

28. The phrase is Lemaître's. See p. 58.

29. Haillant, p. 132.

Chapter Three

1. See Bruno Bettelheim's discussion of this point in *The Uses of Enchantment* (New York: Alfred A. Knopf, 1976), p. 24.

2. Lemaître, p. 109.

3. Ibid., p. 110.

4. Jacques Barchilon, *Le Conte merveilleux français de 1690 à 1790* (Paris: Honoré Champion, 1975), p. 86.

5. Odette de Mourgues, *La Fontaine: Fables*. Studies in French Literature No. 4 (Great Neck, N.Y.: Barron's Educational Series Inc., 1960), p. 27.

6. Léon Boulvé, *De l'Hellénisme chez Fénelon* (1897; rpt. Geneva: Slatkine, 1970), p. 267. Hereafter cited as Boulvé.

7. Madeleine Daniélou, *Fénelon et le Duc de Bourgogne* (Paris: Bloud et Gay, 1955), p. 98.

8. Lemaître, p. 113.

9. Boulvé, pp. 272–74.

10. See, for example, G. Saillard, *Essai sur la fable en France au dix-huitième siècle* (Toulouse: Edouard Privat, 1912), p. 20; and Alfred Lombard, *Fénelon et le retour à l'antique au XVIIIᵉ siècle* (Neuchatel: Secrétariat de l'Université, 1954), p. 67. Hereafter referred to as Lombard.

11. Isabelle Jan, *On Children's Literature,* ed. Catherine Storr (New York: Schocken Books, 1974), p. 16.

12. John W. Cosentini, "The Literary Art of Fénelon's *Dialogues des Morts,*" *Thought Patterns,* 6 (1959), 33. Hereafter referred to as Cosentini.

13. Cosentini, p. 41.

14. Ibid., p. 42.

15. Robert Paul Holley, "Les Dialogues des Morts" from Boileau to the Prince de Ligne: A Study in Form," Diss. Yale 1971, p. 27. Hereafter referred to as Holley.

16. These two dialogues were reprinted in Monville's *Vie de Mignard* in 1730.

17. Cosentini, p. 45.

18. Ibid., p. 38.

19. Goré, *L'Itinéraire,* pp. 468–69.

20. Gustave Lanson, *Histoire illustrée de la littérature française* (Paris: Hachette, 1923), II, 17.

21. Cf. Goré, *L'Itinéraire,* p. 76.

22. Cosentini, p. 49.

23. Jean de La Fontaine, *Oeuvres complètes,* ed. René Gros et Jacques Schiffrin (Paris: Gallimard, 1968), I, 781.

24. Cosentini, p. 51.

25. Ibid., p. 51.

26. Quoted from Le Dieu's *Journal* by Albert Delplanque in *La Pensée de Fénelon* (Paris: Desclée de Brouwer, 1930), p. 76.

27. Johan S. Egilsrud, *Le "Dialogue des Morts dans les littératures française, allemande et anglaise* (Paris: L'Entente Linotypiste, 1934), p. 67. Hereafter cited as Egilsrud.

28. See Lombard, pp. 67–68.

29. Egilsrud, p. 67.

30. Cosentini, p. 48.

31. Ibid., p. 60.

32. Holley, p. 25.

33. Ibid., p. 28.

34. Cosentini, p. 56.

35. Holley, p. 29. Cf. John W. Cosentini, *Fontenelle's Art of Dialogue* (New York: King's Crown Press, 1952), p. 174.

36. Viscount St. Cyres, *François de Fénelon* (London: Methuen and Co., 1901), pp. 80–81. Hereafter referred to as St Cyres.

Chapter Four

1. Roger Bastide, *Les Problèmes de la vie mystique* (Paris: A. Colin, 1931), p. 30.

2. For a more complete treatment of this background material see Louis

Cognet, *Crépuscule des mystiques* (Tournai: Desclée, 1958), pp. 9–55. Hereafter referred to as Cognet, *Crépuscule*.

3. This introductory material is based in part on Gabriel Joppin, *Fénelon et la mystique du pur amour* (Paris: Gabriel Beauchesne et ses fils, 1938), pp. 11–46. Hereafter referred to as Joppin, *Fénelon et la mystique*.

4. Cognet, *Crépuscule*, p. 24.

5. Quoted and discussed by Joppin, *Fénelon et la mystique*, p. 34.

6. Guerrier, pp. 123–25.

7. Jean-Robert Armogathe, *Le Quiétisme* (Paris: Presses Universitaires de France, 1973), p. 5.

8. Guerrier, p. 132.

9. Joppin, *Fénelon et la mystique*, p. 49.

10. Louis Cognet, "La Spiritualité de Madame Guyon," *XVIIe Siècle*, Nos. 12–14 (1951–52), p. 211. Hereafter cited as Cognet, "La Spiritualité."

11. Goré, *L'Itinéraire*, p. 360.

12. Cognet, "La Spiritualité," p. 273.

13. Goré, *L'Itinéraire*, p. 362.

14. Cognet, "La Spiritualité," p. 275.

15. Fénelon, *Explication des articles d'Issy*, ed. Albert Cherel (Paris: Hachette, 1915), p. xiv. Hereafter referred to as *Articles d'Issy*.

16. Goré, *L'Itinéraire*, p. 369.

17. Gabriel Joppin, "Fénelon et le quiétisme," *XVIIe Siècle*, Nos. 12–14 (1951–52), p. 219.

18. First published by Paul Masson in 1907.

19. Fénelon, *Mémoire sur l'état passif*, ed. Jeanne-Lydie Goré in *La Notion d'indifférence chez Fénelon et ses sources* (Paris: Presses Universitaires de France, 1956), p. 207. Hereafter referred to as Goré, *Mémoire*.

20. Goré, *Mémoire*, p. 212.

21. Fénelon, *Le Gnostique de Saint Clément d'Alexandrie*, ed. Paul Dudon (Paris: Gabriel Beauchesne, 1930), p. 58. Hereafter referred to as Dudon.

22. Dudon, pp. 254–55.

23. Ibid., p. 25.

24. Ibid., p. 9.

25. Albert Cherel, *Fénelon et la religion du pur amour* (Paris: Denoël et Steele, 1934), p. 104.

26. *Articles d'Issy*, p. XI.

27. Ibid., pp. 34–35.

28. Ibid., p. 36–37.

29. Fénelon, *Explication des maximes des saints sur la vie intérieure*, ed. Albert Cherel (Paris: Bloud et Cie, 1911), p. 98. Hereafter cited as *Maximes des Saints*.

30. *Maximes des saints*, pp. 103–4.

31. Ibid., p. 105.

32. Joppin, *Fénelon et la mystique,* p. 104.

33. *Maximes des saints,* p. 169.

34. Ibid., p. 301.

35. Ibid., p. 244.

36. Ibid., p. 262.

37. Ibid., p. 302.

38. Carcassonne, *Fénelon,* p. 53.

39. *Maximes des saints,* p. 104.

40. Carcassonne, *Fénelon,* p. 57.

41. Ibid., pp. 62–63.

42. Jacques-Bénigne Bossuet, *Oeuvres complètes* (Paris: Librairie de Louis Vivès, 1862–66), XX, 168.

43. See Guerrier, pp. 464–65.

44. See the remarks of J. Calvet, *La Littérature religieuse de François de Sales à Fénelon* (Paris: Del Duca, 1956), p. 414. Hereafter cited as Calvet.

Chapter Five

1. Cahen, *Télémaque,* I, XXXI.

2. For the material on the sources I have relied primarily on Cahen, *Télémaque,* I, XXXI-II; and Charles Dédéyan, *Le Télémaque de Fénelon* (Paris: Centre de Documentation Universitaire, 1958), pp. 48–50.

3. Cahen, *Télémaque,* I, XXXII.

4. Ibid., XXXIII.

5. Carcassonne, *Fénelon,* p. 79.

6. Alfred Adler, "Fénelon's Télémaque: Intention and Effect," *Studies in Philology* 55, No. 4 (1958), 598. Hereafter cited as Adler.

7. Dédéyan, p. 78.

8. Lombard, pp. 104–5.

9. Cahen finds, in fact, that this section of Book XVII is, in essence, an abridged version of that treatise. See *Télémaque,* II, 484.

10. Carcassonne, *Fénelon,* p. 80.

11. See Fénelon, *Les Aventures de Télémaque,* ed. Jeanne-Lydie Goré (Paris: Garnier-Flammarion, 1968), p. 41. Hereafter referred to as Goré, *Télémaque.* This view is essentially the same voiced by Albert Cherel, *Fénelon ou la religion,* p. 166; and by Carcassonne, *Fénelon,* p. 81.

12. Lemaître, p. 145.

13. This, at least, is the opinion of Goré. *Télémaque,* p. 44.

14. *Maximes des saints,* p. 225.

15. Mark Poster, *The Utopian Thought of Restif de la Bretonne* (New York: New York University Press, 1971), p. 71.

16. Havens, p. 60.

17. See the discussion of this point in Françoise Gallouédec-Genuys, *Le*

Prince selon Fénelon (Paris: Presses Universitaires de France, 1963), pp. 185–86. Hereafter cited as Gallouédec-Genuys.

18. Pierrre Lorson, "Guerre et Paix chez Fénelon," *XVIIe Siècle*, Nos. 12–14 (1951–52), p. 210.

19. Cahen, *Télémaque*, I, 132.

20. Cited by Albert Cherel, *Fénelon au XVIIIe siècle en France* (1715–1820) (1917; rpt. Geneva: Slatkine, 1970), p. 25. Hereafter referred to as Cherel, *Fénelon au XVIIIe siècle*.

21. Cited by Mary Elizabeth Storer, *La Modes des contes de fées* (1928; rpt. Geneva: Slatkine, 1972), p. 214. See also Cherel, *Fénelon au XVIIIe siècle*, p. 25.

22. Nicholas Boileau, *Oeuvres complètes* (Paris: Gallimard, 1966), pp. 638–39.

23. Marc Soriano, *Guide de littérature pour la jeunesse* (Paris: Flammarion, 1975), p. 252. Henceforth referred to as Soriano.

24. Cherel, *Fénelon au XVIIIe siècle*, p. 326.

25. Ibid., p. 331.

26. Ibid., pp. 471–72; 534–35.

27. Ibid., p. 312.

28. Soriano, p. 252.

29. Adler, p. 595.

30. St. Cyres, p. 189.

31. Tilley, p. 259.

32. Adam, V, 176.

33. Lemaître, p. 131.

34. Goré, *Télémaque*, p. 53.

35. Soriano, p. 253.

36. Ibid., p. 253.

Chapter Six

1. Havens, p. 63.

2. Cahen, *Télémaque*, I, XXVIII; and Henri Guillemin, ed., *Lettre à Louis XIV* (Neuchatel: Ides et Calendes, 1961), pp. 59–60.

3. Cahen, *Télémaque*, I, XXVII.

4. Quoted by Havens, p. 65. See also Janet, p. 146.

5. Havens, p. 65.

6. Lemaître, p. 280.

7. René Faille, "Autour de l'*Examen de conscience pour un roi de Fénelon*," *Revue Française d'Histoire du Livre*, 5, No. 8 (1974), 229–30. The 1734 edition, on orders from Louis XV's minister Cardinal Fleury, was suppressed. In 1747 a London publisher, Clement Davis, brought out an edition in French, *Examen de conscience pour un roi*, which was long considered to be the original.

8. Lemaître, p. 282.

9. Roland Mousnier, "Les Idées politiques de Fénelon," *XVIIe Siècle,* Nos. 12–14 (1951–52), p. 204. Hereafter referred to as Mousnier.

10. Havens, p. 66.

11. See Henri Sée's comment in "Les Idées politiques de Fénelon," *Revue d'histoire moderne et contemporaine,* I (1899–1901), 560. Hereafter referred to as Sée.

12. E. K. Sanders, *Fénelon. His Friends and His Enemies* (London: Longmans, Green, 1901), p. 350. Hereafter referred to as Sanders.

13. Gallouédec-Genuys, pp. 46–47.

14. Haillant, pp. 123–24.

15. Quoted by Carcassonne, *Fénelon,* p. 92.

16. See for example the comments of Janet, pp. 149–50; Gilbert Gidel, *La Politique de Fénelon* (1906; rpt. Geneva: Slatkine, 1971), p. 62.

17. Mousnier, p. 205.

18. Sée, p. 558.

19. Goré, *L'Itinéraire,* p. 689.

20. Mousnier, p. 198.

21. Lemaître, p. 289.

Chapter Seven

1. This is the term Cherel uses in speaking of the *Traité de l'existence de Dieu* and the *Lettres sur divers sujets de métaphysique et de religion.* See Cherel, *Fénelon ou la religion,* p. 200.

2. The date is highly speculative. See Cherel, *Fénelon ou la religion,* p. 200.

3. Cherel, *Fénelon au XVIIIe siècle,* p. 258.

4. Quoted by Sanders, p. 384.

5. See Cherel, *Fénelon au XVIIIe siècle,* pp. 258–65.

6. Carcassonne, *Fénelon,* p. 116.

7. St. Cyres, p. 255.

8. Carcassonne, *Fénelon,* pp. 123–24.

9. Cherel, *Fénelon ou la religion,* p. 204.

10. From the text published by Eugène Griselle in his "Fénelon métaphysicien," *Revue de Philosophie,* (1904), 575.

11. This date is given by Carcassonne, *Etat présent,* p. 111; but only one of the letters (VI) actually bears that specific inscription.

12. Will and Ariel Durant, *The Age of Voltaire* (New York: Simon and Schuster, 1965), p. 19.

13. Paul Vernière, *Spinoza et la pensée française avant la Révolution* (Paris: Presses Universitaires de France, 1954), I, 271.

14. Calvet, p. 418.

15. Carcassonne, *Fénelon,* p. 134.

Chapter Eight

1. *Lettre à l'Académie,* ed. Albert Cahen (1899; rpt. Geneva: Slatkine, 1970), p. IV. Hereafter referred to as Cahen, *Lettre.*

2. J. Lewis May, *Fénelon. A Study* (London: Burns Oates and Washbourne, 1938), p. 168.

3. Ernesta Caldarini points out that Fénelon had introduced into his correspondence certain neologisms. See her edition of the *Lettre à l'Académie* (Geneva: Droz, 1970), p. 36. Hereafter referred to as Caldarini.

4. See M. Horn-Monval, *Répertoire bibliographique des traductions et adaptations françaises du théâtre étranger du XVe siècle à nos jours* (Paris: Centre National de la Recherche Scientifique, 1959), II, 15–17; 51–53.

5. Cahen, *Lettre,* p. XX.

6. Tilley, p. 279.

7. Janet, pp. 174–75.

8. Caldarini, p. 110.

9. Cahen, *Lettre,* p. XXII.

10. For a more detailed account of the quarrel the reader is referred to a classic work on the subject, Hippolyte Rigault's *Histoire de la Querelle des Anciens et Modernes* (Paris: Hachette, 1856).

11. For a discussion of this term see Rémy Saisselin, *The Rule of Reason and the Ruses of the Heart* (Cleveland: The Press of Case Western Reserve University, 1970), pp. 122–31.

12. Goré *L'Itinéraire,* pp. 666–70.

13. George E. B. Saintsbury, *A History of Criticism* (New York: Dodd, Mead, 1902), II, 306.

14. See Lombard's citation, p. 69.

15. Lemaître, p. 304.

16. Adam, V, 178.

17. Ibid., 179.

18. Auguste Bourgoin, *Les Maîtres de la critique au XVIIe siècle* (1889; rpt. Geneva: Slatkine, 1970), p. 317.

Selected Bibliography

PRIMARY SOURCES

A. Collected Works

Oeuvres de M. François de Salignac de La Mothe Fénelon, publiées par l'Abbé Gallard et le Père de Querbeuf. 9 vols. Paris: Didot, 1787–92. The first important collection of Fénelon's works. It also includes Querbeuf's life of the author.

Oeuvres complètes de Fénelon. 35 vols. Versailles: J. A. Lebel, 1820–30. First modern edition and the basis for the more manageable "édition de Paris."

Oeuvres de Fénelon . . . précédées d'études sur sa vie, par Aimé Martin. 3 vols. Paris: Lefèvre, 1835. Volume II contains the *Explication des maximes des saints* missing from previous collections.

Oeuvres complètes de Fénelon . . . précédées de son histoire littéraire par M*** Jean E. A. Gosselin directeur du Séminaire de Saint-Sulpice. 10 vols. Paris: Leroux et Jouby, 1848–52. Not complete since it lacks, among other texts, the *Maximes des saints*. Includes a revision of Cardinal de Bausset's *Histoire de Fénelon*.

Oeuvres choisies, ed. Albert Cherel. Second edition. Paris: Hatier, 1930. Excellent selection of texts. No bibliography but good analysis of texts.

Oeuvres spirituelles, ed. François Varillon. Paris: Aubier, 1954. The introduction is a solid piece of scholarship, and the choice of texts is good.

B. Correspondence, Special Editions, and Translations

Correspondance, ed. A. Caron. 11 vols. Paris: Leclère, 1827–29. Published as a supplement to the Versailles edition.

Correspondance de Fénelon, ed. Jean Orcibal. Paris: Klincksieck, 1972–76. Five volumes of this much-needed new edition have appeared so far.

Les Aventures de Télémaque, ed. Albert Cahen. 2 vols. Paris: Hachette, 1927. Remains the standard edition of this work. Excellent material on sources and historical background as well as bibliographical data relating to editions of *Télémaque*.

Les Aventures de Télémaque, ed. Jeanne-Lydie Goré. Paris: Garnier-

Flammarion, 1968. A compact, one-volume edition with a stimulating introduction; it lacks, however, the critical apparatus of the Cahen edition.

Dialogues on Eloquence. A Translation with an Introduction and Notes by Wilbur Samuel Howell. Princeton, N. J.: Princeton University Press, 1951. Good introduction which includes a discussion of this work's place in the history of rhetoric.

Écrits et lettres politiques, ed. C. Urbain. Paris: Bossard, 1920. Provides valuable historical and bibliographical information through introduction and notes which also explain archaic and technical terms.

Explication des Articles d'Issy, ed. Albert Cherel. Paris: Hachette, 1915. A scholarly edition of a significant work which is omitted from the *Oeuvres complètes*. Includes appendices listing Fénelon's sources for his defense of mystical tradition and "pure love."

Explication des maximes des saints sur la vie intérieure, ed. Albert Cherel. Paris: Bloud, 1911. This fine edition explains, among other things, the relation of this famous, but often misjudged work to the rest of Fénelon's writings.

Fénelon on Education. A Translation of the 'Traité de l'Education des Filles' and Other Documents Illustrating Fénelon's Educational Theories, by H. C. Barnard. Cambridge: The University Press, 1966. Informative introduction and notes but no bibliography.

Le Gnostique de Saint Clément d'Alexandrie, ed. Paul Dudon. Paris: Beauchesne, 1930. Good scholarly edition of one of the early documents of the Quietist controversy. Introduction clarifies the position of Fénelon with regard to Gnosticism.

Lettre à l'Académie, ed. Albert Cahen. 1899; rpt. Geneva: Slatkine, 1970.

Lettre à l'Académie, ed. Ernesta Caldarini. Geneva: Droz, 1970. Carefully annotated edition with an appendix which reproduces the *versions primitives*, typographically disposed to enable the reader to follow Fénelon's modifications.

Lettre à Louis XIV. Préface de Henri Guillemin. Neuchâtel: Ides et Calendes, 1961. Also includes the text of the *Examen de conscience* and the letter to the Duc de Chevreuse (August 4, 1710). Not a true critical edition.

Mémoire sur l'état passif, ed. Jeanne-Lydie Goré in *La Notion d'indifférence chez Fénelon*. Paris: Presses Universitaires de France, 1956. A heretofore unedited version of this text appears as part one of the appendix (pp. 189–243).

SECONDARY SOURCES

ADAM, ANTOINE. *Histoire de la littérature française au XVIIᵉ siècle*. 5 vols. 1949–56; rpt. Paris: Del Duca, 1962–68. Standard literary history for the period. Sound and well-balanced work.

ADLER, ALFRED. "Fénelon's *Télémaque:* Intention and Effect." *Studies in Philology*, 55 (1958), 591–602. Challenges the view that *Télémaque* actually produces its intended effect. Points out the stage-conscious, operatic effects of the work.

BEDOYERE, MICHAEL DE LA. *The Archbishop and the Lady.* London: Collins, 1956. Thoroughly readable account of the Quietist controversy. Short bibliography but no index.

BROGLIE, EMMANUEL. *Fénelon à Cambrai d'après sa correspondance, 1699–1715.* Paris: Plon, 1884. Still the best-known work on this particular phase of Fénelon's life. Little material concerning apologetic activity.

CARCASSONNE, ELY. *Etat présent des travaux sur Fénelon.* Paris: Belles Lettres, 1939. Although in need of updating, it is still an indispensable tool for the student of Fénelon. Complete bibliography except for periodicals.

_____. *Fénelon, l'homme et l'oeuvre.* Paris: Boivin, 1946. Best of the short studies. A scholarly and sensitive approach to the man and his work.

CHEREL, ALBERT. *Fénelon au XVIIIe Siècle en France (1715–1820).* 1917; rpt. Geneva: Slatkine, 1970. A scholarly, detailed study of Fénelon's influence on the eighteenth century and the pre-Romantics. Fine bibliography which includes a listing of editions from 1687–1820.

_____. *Fénelon, ou la religion du pur amour.* Paris: Denoël et Steele, 1934. Strives to give unity and cohesion to Fénelon's life and works by relating them to his attachment to "pure love."

COGNET, LOUIS. *Crépuscule des mystiques.* Tournai: Desclée, 1958. Rich in background information. A fine blend of facts and ideas.

COSENTINI, JOHN W. "The Literary Art of Fénelon's *Dialogues des Morts.*" *Thought Patterns* 6 (1959), 29–61. Concentrates on study of the *Dialogues* from the point of view of form.

DANIÉLOU, MADELEINE. *Fénelon et le Duc de Bourgogne.* Paris: Bloud et Gay, 1955. An historical, psychological approach to the question of Fénelon's role as preceptor. Lively and interesting. Poor bibliography.

GALLOUÉDEC-GENUYS, FRANÇOISE. *Le Prince selon Fénelon.* Paris: Presses Universitaires de France, 1963. Thematic, topical rather than historical approach to Fénelon's views on kingship. Good documentation and bibliography.

GIDEL, GILBERT. *La Politique de Fénelon.* 1906; rpt. Geneva: Slatkine, 1971. Analysis of major political works, but no effort either to synthesize them or situate them historically.

GORÉ, JEANNE-LYDIE. *L'Itinéraire de Fénelon. Humanisme et Spiritualité.* Paris: Presses Universitaires de France, 1957. Dense but impressive study. A well-documented account of Fénelon's aesthetic and spiritual aspirations.

GOUHIER, HENRI. *Fénelon philosophe.* Paris: Librairie Philosophique J.

Vrin, 1977. A clear and perceptive analysis of this aspect of Fénelon's work.

GUERRIER, LOUIS. *Madame Guyon. Sa Vie, sa doctrine et son influence.* 1881; rpt. Geneva: Slatkine, 1971. Overly sympathetic to Madame Guyon, it lacks a certain objectivity. Good documentation in general.

HAILLANT, MARGUERITE. *Fénelon et la prédication.* Paris: Klincksieck, 1969. First complete study of Fénelon's sermons. Excellent chapter on rhetorical background.

HAVENS, GEORGE R. *The Age of Ideas. From Reaction to Revolution in Eighteenth-Century France.* 1955; rpt. New York: The Free Press, 1965. Excellent survey of Fénelon's political ideas and their relation to enlightened thought.

HILLENAAR, HENK. *Fénelon et les Jésuites.* The Hague: Martinus Nijhoff, 1967. Thorough, interesting account of this relationship.

HOLLEY, ROBERT PAUL. "*Les Dialogues des morts* from Boileau to the Prince de Ligne: A Study in Form." Diss. Yale 1971. Well-conceived study which defines Fénelon's place in the dialogue tradition. Emphasizes fictional reality of his treatment.

JANET, PAUL. *Fénelon.* Paris: Hachette, 1892. Rather superficial short study. Ignores much of Fénelon's apologetic work.

JOPPIN, GABRIEL. *Fénelon et la mystique du pur amour.* Paris: Gabriel Beauchesne et ses fils, 1938. Complements Cognet's work. Detailed and informative.

————. "Fénelon et le quiétisme." *XVIIᵉ Siècle,* Nos. 12–14 (1951–52), pp. 215–26. Attempts a new interpretation of the Fénelon-Bossuet conflict. Succeeds in relating Quietism and Jansenism.

LEMAÎTRE, JULES. *Fénelon.* Paris: Arthème Fayard, 1910. Impartial view of Fénelon. Critical insights still merit the reader's attention.

LITTLE, KATHARINE DAY. *François de Fénelon.* New York: Harper and Brothers, 1951. A sympathetic biography which concentrates more on personality than works.

LOMBARD, ALFRED. *Fénelon et le retour à l'antique au XVIIIᵉ siècle.* Neuchâtel: Secrétariat de l'Université, 1954. This fine study concentrates on Fénelon as poet rather than as theologian or mystic. Supplementing Cherel's work, it explains his influence on nineteenth-century writers. Excellent bibliography contained in the notes.

MALLET-JORIS, Françoise. *Jeanne Guyon.* Paris: Flammarion, 1978. A vindication of Madame Guyon's life and activities by a significant modern novelist.

MAY, JAMES LEWIS. *Fénelon. A Study.* London: Burns Oates and Washbourne, 1938. Good from the standpoint of information on personal life of Fénelon. Poorly documented.

MOUSNIER, ROLAND. "Les Idées politiques de Fénelon." *XVIIᵉ Siècle,*

Nos. 12–14 (1951–52), pp. 190–206. Clearly written. Unsympathetic interpretation of Fénelon's political theories.

St. Cyres, Viscount. *François de Fénelon*. London: Methuen, 1901. More critical than Sanders' study. Unsympathetic to mysticism.

Sanders, E. K. *Fénelon. His Friends and His Enemies. 1651–1715*. London: Longmans, Green, 1901. Sympathetic treatment of Fénelon's mysticism. Poorly documented.

Sée, Henri, "Les Idées politiques de Fénelon." *Revue d'Histoire Moderne et Contemporaine* I (1899–1900), pp. 545–65. Interesting contrast of Fénelon and the traditional absolutists of his time.

Tilley, Arthur. *The Decline of the Age of Louis XIV*. 1929; rpt. New York: Barnes and Noble, 1968. Although outdated bibliographically, the section on Fénelon (pp. 244–96) is generally perceptive and clear.

Index

182